JOURNAL OF SEMITIC STUDIES
MONOGRAPH No. 4

THE ARABIC NOVEL
AN HISTORICAL AND CRITICAL INTRODUCTION

BY

ROGER ALLEN

Associate Professor of Arabic in the University of Pennsylvania, Philadelphia

UNIVERSITY OF MANCHESTER 1982

Published by the University of Manchester

First published 1982

Printed in Belgium by the Imprimerie Orientaliste,
Louvain

ISBN 0 9507885 0 3

CONTENTS

For the grandparents of
Marianna and Timothy

PREFACE

The present work represents the fourth of the series of *Journal of Semitic Studies* Monographs, and as with the third one, my own *Al-Maqrīzī's "Book of contention and strife concerning the relations between the Banū Umayya and the Banū Hāshim"* (1980), publication has been made possible through the funds generously supplied by the University of Kuwait for the encouragement of Arabic and Islamic studies in the University of Manchester's Department of Near Eastern Studies. I am accordingly most grateful to the Rector of Kuwait University in thus allowing us to extend the Monograph Series.

As Professor Allen explains in his Introduction (below, p. 9), the genesis of the present work lies in a series of lectures which he gave in the Department of Near Eastern Studies. Those of us present then heard how the novel tradition in the Arab world has grown to maturity in little more than two or three generations. The novels analysed below show many penetrating insights into aspects of contemporary Arab society: in the macrocosm, the splendours and miseries of its adjustment to the larger world, and the counter-movement of its rejection and withdrawal from it; in the microcosm, the struggle of the individual against the constrictions of society, of the village, or of the family, a struggle in which the protagonist may well appear as the *khārijī*, that archetypical figure of recent Western literature, the outsider.

It is accordingly hoped that this book will assist in making better known to the Western world these remarkable achievements of the present, vigorous generation of Arab writers.

C.E. Bosworth

Manchester, July 1981

ABBREVIATIONS EMPLOYED

EI[2]	*Encyclopaedia of Islam*, Second edition
IC	*Islamic Culture*
JAL	*Journal of Arabic Literature*
JAOS	*Journal of the American Oriental Society*
JARCE	*Journal of the American Research Center in Egypt*
MEJ	*Middle East Journal*

INTRODUCTION

This work was first presented in the form of a series of three lectures which were given at the University of Manchester in May, 1980. The invitation to give those lectures (made possible through funds provided by the University of Kuwait) and to expand them into the present format came from Professor Edmund Bosworth, the Professor of Arabic Studies at the University of Manchester. I would like to take this opportunity of thanking him and his colleagues on the editorial staff of the *Journal of Semitic Studies* for giving me this opportunity to publish my views on the Arabic novel at such welcome length.

The novel in the Arab world has been the subject of numerous studies, but, with a few notable exceptions, they have not matched the quantity or quality of those on poetry. It may perhaps be suggested that this situation reflects the age-old love of the Arabs for poetry which extends back to the beginnings of Arabic literature as it has come down to us. In the modern period, for example, there are now available a large number of studies in European languages on modern Arabic poetry, and three complete studies in English, each of which approaches the subject from a different point of view. In the realm of the novel, studies in English tend to concentrate on a single country (especially Egypt, for reasons which will be discussed below) or a single author. Surveys of the novel as it has developed throughout the Arab world are much rarer and are in the main confined to those in the Arabic language.

It is my perception of the current situation with regard to the study of the Arabic novel which has led me to attempt this introductory survey of the genre and its development. It should be made clear from the outset—and indeed it is reasonably obvious—that the novel is too complex a phenomenon and the Arab world is too large a geographical entity for this work to be anything more than an introduction to the subject. The larger study of the Arabic novel, its development and basic features, remains to be written. If others share my belief that the Arabic novel has achieved a true maturity and sense of identity since the Second World War, then they may perhaps be prepared to concede also that a slightly longer period of creativity in this genre, along with the preparation of a number of preliminary studies (of which the present volume hopes to be one), will make the writing of a much needed longer study of the Arabic novel from the critical and historical points of view both more feasible and useful.

The format of the present work follows that of the original lectures reasonably closely. I should point out immediately that the word "Arabic" in the title of the book refers to the language; my subject is works of narrative fiction which have been written in the Arabic language. I am aware that the equivalent epithet in Arabic, namely *'arabī*, can refer to both people and language, but in this instance I will not be dealing, for example, with the large number of works written by the Francophone authors of the Maghrib, such as Muḥammad Dīb, al-Khaṭībī, and Kātib Yāsīn. For, while their names are unmistakably Arab, their writings are not only in the French language but show a clear affinity with the traditions of contemporary French literature, as a writer such as al-Khaṭībī readily admits. At my own university, the works of such authors are read in the French section of the Department of Romance Languages. Nor will I be dealing in detail with works which have been written by Arabs in other languages.

The first chapter begins with a discussion of the novel as a genre and surveys various attempts which have been made to define it. The origins of the genre are then investigated as a prelude to and in connection with the discussion of the narrative tradition in Arabic literature during the classical period. The second chapter traces the beginnings of the modern Arabic renaissance, and particularly those aspects most germane to the development of a tradition of prose fiction, and then the early attempts at fiction are surveyed until the outset of the Second World War. The period of maturity in the Arabic novel is the subject of the next chapter in which the different types of novel, varied in theme, style, narrative approach, political motivation and country of origin, all written between 1939 and the present day (1980), are analysed. The fourth chapter consists of a series of discrete analyses of a number of novels which have been selected from the vast corpus of works in this genre because I find them excellent examples of the wealth of novelistic output in the Arab world in recent decades. It is a fitting sign of that wealth that other critics have chosen and can choose an entirely different selection of their own, one which would, no doubt, reflect their own national origins, education, biases and interests, just as my own selection certainly reflects mine. My only hope is that no one will wish to claim that any of the works which I have chosen is an inferior contribution to the tradition of the Arabic novel.

I expressed above the hope that this work might serve as a contribution to further research into the vast and variegated field of Arabic fiction. It would also be a source of great satifaction for me if this survey were also able to introduce the Arabic novelistic tradition to that much wider Western audience who have in general had little access to what it has to offer; all varieties of literature study, and particularly the comparative dimension, would seem to be liable to benefit from such access. In writing this book I have made every effort to keep technical terminology in Arabic to a minimum, but inevitably some words have crept in. To assist and encourage this hoped-for wider audience I now append a short glossary of Arabic terms which are found in the text:

ʿaraq: a strong, colourless liquor often diluted with water; akin to the Greek ouzo.

kaffiyya: the headdress worn in many Arab countries, often used as protection against the sun and/or sand.

mahjar: the name given to the school of littérateurs who settled in the Americas during the late nineteenth and early twentieth centuries; their acknowledged leader was Jubrān Khalīl Jubrān.

maqāma: a prose genre in Arabic literature combining verbal virtuosity with a picaresque portrayal of society. It was almost certainly used for the first time by Badīʿ al-Zamān al-Hamadhānī (d. 1008).

muftī: someone who delivers *fatwās* or legal opinions.

nahḍa: the Arabic word for "renaissance, rebirth."

qaṣīda: usually translated as "ode," the Arabic word used to describe the polythematic poem in classical Arabic literature, the earliest examples of which date from the sixth century A.D.

qiṣṣa: "story," normally used with the adjective *qaṣīra* ("short") to describe the short story genre. See p. 93, n. 99.

riwāya: literally "narrative," but now used by the majority of Arabi critics as "novel." See p. 93, n. 99.

saj': a style of prose exploiting the potentialities of Arabic morphology to produce rhyming patterns, often with great lexical virtuosity. Found in much Arabic prose from an early age (including the Quran itself), it is particularly associated with the *maqāma* genre (see above).

sīra [*sha'biyya*]: popular folk tale (e.g. those of Antar, Baybars, the Banī Hilāl, etc.)

'umda: the head of the village community in Egypt, selected from among the local influential families. The position was used by Egyptian littérateurs as a butt for jokes concerning both corruption and rustic naïveté.

CHAPTER I

THE NOVEL: DEFINITIONS AND ORIGINS

Unassisted by established critical traditions, faced with chaotic diversity among the things called novels, critics of fiction have been driven to invent an order of some kind, even at the expense of being dogmatic. "Great traditions" of innumerable shapes and sizes, based on widely divergent universal qualities, have in consequence been discovered and abandoned with appalling rapidity. The novel began, we are told, with Cervantes, with Defoe, with Fielding, with Richardson, with Jane Austen—or was it with Homer? It was killed by Joyce, by Proust, by the rise of symbolism, by the loss of respect for—or was it the excessive absorption with?—hard facts. No, no, it still lives, but only in the work of...Thus, on and on.

In this passage, Wayne C. Booth shows us clearly how difficult it has been and is to provide universal definitions when dealing with the novel.[1] The death of the genre has been proclaimed on many occasions and denied just as often, as in an article in *The Economist* of February 1970.[2] Almost from the outset the genre has lived up to the element of "newness", "difference", implicit in the origins of the word "novel" itself. E.M. Forster describes it for us in his own unique way:

...the novel is a formidable mass, and it is so amorphous...most distinctly one of the moister areas of literature—irrigated by a thousand rills and occasionally degenerating into a swamp.[3]

while, within a more strictly definitional environment, M.J. Abrams observes, with not a little implicit resignation:

... the term novel is now applied to a great variety of writings that have in common only the attribute of being extended works of prose fiction.[4]

Relatively few Arab critics have investigated the terms of reference of the novel genre in general and outside its particular Arab-world context. One such is the Palestinian poet, novelist, artist and critic, Jabrā Ibrāhīm Jabrā, who has, among other

1 *The rhetoric of fiction*, Chicago: University of Chicago Press, 1961, 36.
2 "The novel is not dead", *The Economist*, 14 February 1970, 40-1.
3 *Aspects of the novel*, London: Penguin Books, 1966, 13.
4 *A Glossary of literary terms*, New York: Holt, Rinehart and Winston, 1971, 110.

things, translated the work of Shakespeare, William Faulkner and Sir James Frazer into Arabic. His collections of critical articles contain a number of studies of the novel, its development, form and origins. In that we will be examining one of his novels in the fourth chapter, his views on the genre as a whole are of considerable interest.

In an article entitled "The human novel", he suggests that the novel is a fusion of various elements drawn from the Aristotelian categories: from the tradition of tragedy, it takes the major theme of the conflict of the individual with forces more powerful than himself, something which he traces from Aeschylus to Dostoevsky and Faulkner; the epic supplies such themes as the clash of the individual with society, betrayal, envy, chivalry, and so on; from the dramatic comes the concern with the portrayal of situations and emotions, and in particular, the characterisation of individuals through dialogue.[5] The beginnings of the genre are traced back to the mediaeval romance (it will be recalled that the word for "novel" in both French and German is "roman") in which the knight sallies forth to combat the forces of evil. With the passage of time and the transformation of society, the venue changes from castle and forest to society and the city. With the appearance of Romanticism, the novel takes up the cause of freedom of the individual and social justice. The emergence of a middle class and its aspirations for a better life, the acquisition of material goods and money, these topics give the realistic novelist a wide scope to describe in vivid detail the rise and decline of families within the social spectrum. More recently, Jabrā notes, the focus has shifted from an investigation of society and its conflicts to another kind of complex maze, that of the inner self of man, as novelists probe the secrets of his conscience using the techniques of modern psychology on the scientific plane and stream-of-consciousness and interior monologue on the more literary level.

This modern novelistic tradition shares with other manifestations of art in the modern world an unwillingness to be governed or trammelled by any preconceived notions regarding

[5] "al-Riwāya al-insāniyya", in *al-Ḥurriyya wa-al-ṭūfān*, Beirut: Dār Majallat Shiʿr, 1960, 58 ff. These connections are explored further by Georg Lukacs, *The theory of the novel*, trans. Anna Bostock, Cambridge, Mass.: MIT Press, 1977 (esp. Chs. 2 and 3); and Ian Watt, *The rise of the novel*, London: Penguin Books, 1966 (esp. 9 ff.).

form, style or indeed almost any other aspect of the creative act. The concept of "newness" to which we referred above calls to mind the writings of one modern Arab intellectual in particular, the Syrian-Lebanese poet Adūnīs ('Alī Aḥmad Sa'īd). He regards the primary function of poetry as being to innovate, to use words in new and unfamiliar ways. In his own words:

New poetry ... is a vision, and vision by its very nature is a leap outside of normal concepts. Thus it is a change in the order of things and in the way of looking at them. Modern poetry then is a revolt against old poetic forms and methods, a rejection of attitudes and styles whose goals are no longer to be found.[6]

This particular quotation comes from a work devoted to poetry, but the import of its message and the possibility of its transfer to the terms of reference for other genres is clear enough. Furthermore, Adūnīs himself has actively encouraged a new approach to the evaluation of Arabic belles-lettrist prose in a series of articles published in the literary magazine of which he is an editor, *Mawāqif*.

In the realm of poetry, Adūnīs's efforts can be placed into the context of a continuous chain of developments, experiments and "*ruptures*" which can be traced back to the early efforts of the neo-classicists in the nineteenth century. These poets reestablished the canons and norms of the great poetic tradition of many centuries earlier and thus provided an indigenous entity on which later generations could build. In the realm of prose, the progress has been both slower and more variegated. The primary factors involved in this differing process of development can effectively be narrowed down firstly to the influence of Western genres and the need to adapt them to both language and societal circumstances, and secondly to the nature of the precedents which existed in the classical prose tradition.

With regard to the Arabic novel, there is fairly general agreement among critics that its origins lie in the Western traditions. Charles Vial, for example, says as much in unequivocal terms:

The modern *ḳiṣṣa* owes nothing to Arab tradition. It is linked neither with the folklore of the *Thousand and one nights* nor with tales of chivalry nor with narratives of *adab*.[7]

[6] Adūnīs, *Zaman al-shi'r*, Beirut: Dār al-'Awda, 1972, 9.
[7] Art. "Ḳiṣṣa", in *EI*², Leiden: E. J. Brill, 1954-, in progress.

And yet, such a categorical and dogmatic statement as this ignores certain subtleties of tradition and cultural interchange. For, while the influence of the famous *Thousand and one nights* on the emerging novelistic tradition in the Arab world may be minimal, the same cannot be said of the impact of several of the popular folktale traditions on Europe in the eighteenth century and thereafter, of which Rimsky-Korsakov's *Scheherezade* and *Antar Symphony* are merely tokens. It is, in fact, rather ironical that the *Thousand and one nights*, the most famous work of Arabic literature, should have had such a tremendous impact on Europe at the time of its translation by Galland (1703-13),[8] while its status as popular literature has until recently cast it into what one critic has termed "that critical netherland of Middle Arabic and dialect 'non-literature',"[9] and has thus kept it almost *hors-de-combat* in the early stages of the development of a tradition of modern Arabic fiction. Jabrā Ibrāhīm Jabrā himself is one of those critics who emphasise that the use of multi-layered techniques, the fragmentation of time, the concern with the life of the individual in society—all major concerns of the contemporary novel—are present in the *Thousand and one nights*. Leaving aside the fascinating formal complexities and moral message of such tales as that of Sindbad the Sailor,[10] one can point to the tale of the Three Apples as an almost classic detective novel: the dead body is found at the beginning of the story, the Caliph wants to find out who the culprit is, and in the end, the entire sorry tale is unravelled. The literary qualities of this vast store of mediaeval Arabic popular literature are only just beginning to be explored and analysed. Meanwhile, it is sufficient to observe that the *Thousand and one nights* and other popular *sīra* traditions seem to offer a fertile area of investigation into possible precedents to the modern narrative prose tradition in Arabic, as Jabrā points out.[11] The Iraqi critic, Ṣafā' al-Khulūṣī, even sees a close relationship between the appear-

[8] See C. Knipp, "The *Arabian Nights* in England: Galland's translation and its successors", *JAL* V (1974), 44-54.

[9] See Bridget Connelly, "The structure of four Bani Hilal tales", *JAL* IV (1973), 18-47.

[10] See Peter Molan, "Sinbad the Sailor, a commentary on the ethics of violence", *JAOS* XCVIII/3 (July-Sept., 1978), 237-47.

[11] See *Yanābī' al-ru'yā*, Beirut: al-Mu'assasa al-'Arabiyya, 1979, 68-71; 'Abbās Khiḍr, "al-Mūnūlūg al-dākhilī fī Alf Layla wa-Layla", *al-'Arabī* (Aug. 1980), 120-2.

ance of a translation of the *Thousand and one nights* in English and the emergence of the modern novel.[12]

In anticipation of further research on the popular literature of the Islamic Middle Ages, such conclusions may seem somewhat premature. More acceptable in present circumstances is the statement of Edward Said:

The twentieth-century novel in Arabic has a variety of forbears, none of them formally and dynastically prior and useful as, say, in the rather directly useful way that Fielding antedates Dickens. Arabic literature before the twentieth century has a rich assortment of narrative forms—*qissa*, *sīra*, *hadīth*, *khurāfa*, *ustūra*, *khabar*, *nādira*, *maqāma*—of which no one seems to have become, as the European novel did, the major narrative type.[13]

However, as these rich and exciting possibilities continue to be investigated, the tradition of the Arabic novel proceeds with its own momentum. To some novelists in the Arab world the Western provenance of the novel is accepted; consider for example the words of ʿAbd al-Raḥmān Munīf, one of a younger generation of novelists whose work will be considered in chapter four:

The Arabic novel has no heritage. Thus, any contemporary Arab novelist has to look for a means of expression for himself, with hardly any guidance to aid him. It is thus inevitable that he will make some mistakes and display shortcomings.[14]

Fortunately, this willingness to acknowledge a debt to the West on the matter of the novel has in no way inhibited the creativity of Arab writers; the basic question has been one of "catching up", as both Najīb Maḥfūẓ, the Arab world's most famous novelist, and Jabrā have pointed out.[15] In any case, such writers can, no doubt, take comfort from the statement of Jacques Berque that:

... the genealogies of creativity do not, and need not, follow a straight line. The history and variations of artistic genius presuppose dis-

[12] S.A. Khulusi, "Modern Arabic fiction with special reference to Iraq", *IC* XXX (1956), 199-210.

[13] Introd. to Ḥalīm Barakāt, *Days of dust*, trans. Trevor Le Gassick, Wilmette, Illinois: Medina Press International, 1974, p. xiii.

[14] *al-Maʿrifa* (Feb., 1979), 193.

[15] For Maḥfūẓ, see *al-Marāyā*, Cairo: Maktabat Miṣr, 1972, 66, and *Mirrors*, trans. Roger Allen, Chicago: Bibliotheca Islamica, 1977, 42; for Jabrā, see "Modern Arabic literature and the West", *JAL* II (1971), 76-91, and *Yanābīʿ al-ruʾyā*, 138.

continuity, interaction, an unexpected intersection of lineages rather than a simple linear succession. Why look among the *ta'ziyas*, popular skits, or magic lantern shows for the ancestors of the contemporary theatre if the latter does no more than provide a modern language to life's theatricality that formerly assumed quite different forms?[16]

With the benefit of hindsight we may observe that, in the period following the Second World War, the tradition of the Arabic novel remained essentially unaffected by the few gestures of neoclassicism in prose. While it may be true that, during the transitional stage at the beginning of this century, there were distinct echoes of earlier types of Arabic prose, the novel tradition turned its back on such conscious archaisms, which in any case failed to survive for any length of time because no one genre could predominate in the same way that the *qaṣīda* could at the hands of the neo-classical poets.

This said, however, it should also be observed that, while the novel tradition has indeed drawn most of its inspiration from Western models, a number of writers and especially critics have been reinvestigating the nature of narrative in the mediaeval tradition of popular prose—we would cite Suhayr al-Qalamāwī and Fārūq Khūrshīd, in addition to Jabrā. Some recent novels and writings on this genre suggest that an increasing national consciousness and a greater familiarity with the classical prose tradition may lead, at least in the works of some contemporary novelists, to a closer association between the novel today and the older imaginative narratives which were apparently ignored in the earlier stages of the development of the Arabic novel.

[16] *Cultural expression in Arab society today*, Austin: University of Texas Press, 1978, 200, cf. 259-60.

CHAPTER II

THE EARLY DEVELOPMENT OF THE ARABIC NOVEL TRADITION

Contemporary Arabic literature is the result of a long but often accelerated process which has its basis in the *nahḍa*, the movement of cultural revival or renaissance which began in earnest during the nineteenth century, although some of its roots can be traced to an earlier period. This phenomenon varied widely in its course and impact within the different regions of the Arabic-speaking world, but in every case the particular local development was the result of a process which involved two principal forces. These are variously known as the old and the new, the traditional and the modern, the classicists and the modernists, and so on; more specifically, the encounter with the West, its science and culture, on the one hand, and the rediscovery and stimulation of the great classical heritage of the Arabic language and its literature, on the other.

Much of the pioneering work in this latter aspect was carried out by members of the Christian families in what was then called Syria but now combines both Syria and Lebanon. These communities had been in contact with the West, and especially Rome and France, for a large part of that period which has been dubbed "the period of decadence," a title of rather dubious validity in my estimation in view of the almost total dearth of knowledge about the literature of the period, of which the popular tales mentioned above are just one example.[1] Connections with the Roman Catholic Church were firmly established and were reflected in the educational opportunities available. This missionary and educational activity intensified in the nineteenth century when Protestant missionaries began to arrive, and notably some from the United States. A Bible translation project was merely one manifestation of these new contacts, and in 1866 the Syrian Protestant College was founded in Beirut, an institution which, under its more familiar modern

[1] See the article on the *'aṣr al-inḥiṭāṭ* by Shukrī Fayṣal, in al-'Alī, Ṣāliḥ, *et al.*, *al-Adab al-'Arabī fī āthār al-dārisīn*, Beirut: Dār al-'Ilm li-al-Malāyīn, 1971.

title, the American University in Beirut, has played a notable role in the fostering of education and culture in the region and the Arab world as a whole.

A whole series of families—the Bustānīs, Yāzijīs, Shidyāqs, Naqqāshs, and so on—were now to make notable contributions to the process of reviving among the Arabs an awareness of the riches of their own language and its literature. To cite just a few examples: Buṭrus al-Bustānī (1819-83) came under the influence of Cornelius van Dyke, an American missionary, and helped in the translation of the Bible into Arabic. He also wrote a dictionary, *Muḥīṭ al-muḥīṭ*, and the larger part of an encyclopaedia, *Dā'irat al-ma'ārif*, on which he was working at the time of his death. Nāṣīf al-Yāzijī (1800-71) read the *maqāmāt* of the eleventh century prose writer al-Ḥarīrī in the French edition of Sylvestre de Sacy and was thus inspired to write a set of his own entitled *Majma' al-baḥrayn* which do indeed have al-Ḥarīrī's *maqāmāt* as their model in that the emphasis is on verbal artistry and virtuosity to the almost total exclusion of any concern with content, thus sacrificing the somewhat picaresque and entertaining qualities of al-Ḥarīrī's own model and predecessor, Badī' al-Zamān al-Hamadhānī. Mārūn al-Naqqāsh (1817-55) returned from a period spent in Italy full of ideas about the drama and proceeded to adapt the plays of Molière, the first of which was produced on a stage in his own house in 1848.[2] Aḥmad Fāris al-Shidyāq (1804-87) described his own visit to Europe in his *al-Sāq 'alā al-sāq fīmā huwa al-Fāryāq*, an untranslatable title which contains a pun of his own name (in that Fāryāq includes the first syllable of Fāris and the last of Shidyāq) as well as constituting an excellent demonstration of the revival of the proclivity of mediaeval Arabic prose for rhyming titles. The work includes some vitriolic tirades against the Christian clergy in Lebanon, which is hardly surprising in view of the fact that Shidyāq's brother, As'ad, was hounded to death by the Maronite Patriarch for converting to Protestantism. The echoes of this event and others like it can still be felt in the early fiction of Jubrān Khalīl Jubrān which we will discuss below.[3]

These are just a few examples of the wealth of activity which

[2] See Matti Moosa, "Naqqāsh and the rise of the native Arab theatre in Syria", *JAL* III (1972), 106-17.

[3] Khalīl Hāwī, *Kahlil Gibran, his background, character and works*, Beirut: The American University of Beirut Oriental Series, no. 41, 1963, 43.

was taking place in Syria and Lebanon during the nineteenth century, at least until the vicious decade of the 1850s. During that period, civil war broke out in the region, a tragedy which culminated in the massacre of a large number of Christians in Damascus in 1860.[4] At this, a large number of Christian families decided to leave; some went to Egypt, while others travelled still further, coming to Europe and the Americas, in the latter case forming the basis for one of the most important schools in modern Arabic literature, the *mahjar* or emigré school.

It is hardly surprising that, in the wake of this exodus, the movement of cultural revival in Syria and Lebanon should have slowed down somewhat. In any case, this tragic set of circumstances was not the only factor involved. For the area was under the strict control of the Ottoman government in Istanbul, and the dissemination of written materials was made yet more difficult by the problems of censorship which are well characterised for us by Muḥammad Kurd ʿAlī in his *Memoirs*:

> What pained me most was the heavy censorship and the complications involved in obtaining the permit for publication ... There was nothing to go on in censorship except the whim of the censor ... How often I suffered from the publisher's deletion of whole paragraphs of mine, and sometimes entire articles.[5]

Much the some situation prevailed to the east in Iraq. The travels of the two Iraqi poets, al-Ruṣāfī and al-Zahāwī in search of work and/or publication opportunities show clearly the authority of the Ottoman administration over the region and particularly the power of censorship in Iraq. As Salmā al-Jayyūsī has shown in her recent survey of modern Arabic poetry,[6] the geographical position of the country did not encourage the same kinds of contact with Europe as can be seen in other parts of the Middle East, and the traditional types of poetry held sway in the region. In view of these facts it is not surprising both that Iraq has been a major centre of poetic activity and innovation throughout the modern period and that an Iraqi fictional tradition developed relatively later than was

[4] Albert Hourani, *Arabic thought in the liberal age*, London: Oxford University Press, 1962, 61-4.

[5] Trans. Khalil Totah, Washington: American Council of Learned Societies, 1954, 13.

[6] *Trends and movements in modern Arabic poetry*, Leiden: E.J. Brill, 1977, I, 26.

the case elsewhere. It should be added immediately that any time lag which may have existed at some point in the developmental process has long since been eradicated, and Iraqi novelists today are in the forefront, from the viewpoints both of creativity and of experiment, as later chapters will illustrate.

An area of the Arabic-speaking world whose literature has been largely neglected by both Arab and Western scholars is the Maghrib and Tunisia.[7] We have noted above that the Francophone authors of the area do not fall within our purview, but there have been and are a number of writers who express themselves in Arabic; indeed, certain countries have recently been making particular efforts to encourage and foster literature in Arabic during the post-colonial era of the 1960s and 1970s.

If Iraq suffered from a certain geographical separation from the centres of revival in the nineteenth century, the same is true to an even greater degree of Morocco, Algeria and Tunisia. Rizzitano notes that

> Il Marocco, infatti, rimasto fuori dal blocco del territori arabofoni languenti sotto l'egemonia dell'impero ottomano[8]

but that very fact must have been among the factors which led France to colonise neighbouring Algeria, beginning in 1830. The relative proximity to France itself and economic conditions in the home country seemed to have encouraged the French to embark on a large-scale venture in economic and cultural imperialism:

> Les Français ne se bornèrent pas à occuper militairement l'Algérie, ils s'efforcèrent de la dominer économiquement et culturellement, afin que leurs positions dans ce pays fussent vraiment solides. Les écoles arabes en Algérie furent fermées, la possibilité d'acquérir un enseignement arabe était systématiquement limitée et empêchée, tandis qu'avec l'accroissement de nombre d'immigrants français, l'influence de la langue française et de l'enseignement français était sans cesse renforcée.[9]

In 1881, one year before the British occupation of Egypt, the

[7] As is noted by ʿAbdallāh Kannūn, *Aḥādīth ʿan al-adab al-Maghribī al-ḥadīth*, Cairo; Maʿhad al-Dirāsāt al-ʿArabiyya al-ʿĀliya, 1964, 6.

[8] Umberto Rizzitano, "Il 'racconto' (*qiṣṣah*) nella narrativa araba contemporana del Marocco", *Atti del terzo congresso di studi arabi e islamici, Ravello*, Naples: Istituto Universitario Orientale, Napoli, 1967, 569-93.

[9] Svetozar Pantucek, *La littérature algérienne moderne*, Prague: Academia, 1969, 21-2.

French occupied Tunisia. The process of revival had progressed somewhat further here, due in no small part to the ideas and actions of Khayr al-Dīn Pāshā and also the influence of Muḥammad ʿAbduh, the great Egyptian reformer.[10] Thus Islamic education was able to survive and even live alongside the influx of French culture and indeed produce in Abū al-Qāsim al-Shābbī one of the modern period's most fiery and eloquent romantic poets. It has to be admitted however that figures like al-Shābbī are exceptionally rare in the development of modern literature in the Maghrib; the pervasive influence of French culture and the conservative nature of such Islamic education as did exist made such a situation almost inevitable. The nineteenth century, a period of such development in other parts of the Arabic speaking world, forms part of the "pre-history" of the renaissance in the Maghrib.[11] The real developments in Arabic fiction in this area come in the twentieth century, and particularly, following the achievement of independence from France, when writing in Arabic begins to be encouraged.

It is probably in Egypt that the effect of the impact of the West is most immediately evident. When Napoleon invaded the country in 1798, the Egyptians were brought face to face with European advances in technology and military science, and, in the wake of their defeat, with the wonders of European culture and scientific knowledge. Following the French withdrawal, Muḥammad ʿAlī sent missions to Italy and later to France to study military tactics and weapons procedures; along with the first such mission to France went Rifāʿa Rāfiʿ al-Ṭahṭāwī (1801-73) as *imām*. He learned French and studied the culture, political system and habits of the French in some detail, recording his impressions in his famous work *Takhlīṣ al-ibrīz fī talkhīṣ Bārīz*. This is, in fact, the first in a whole series of works in which Arab visitors to Europe have recorded their impressions; we have already mentioned al-Shidyāq's contribution. In fact, this subject has served as the framework for a series of novels which have appeared during the course of the twentieth century by Tawfīq al-Ḥakīm, Ṭāhā Ḥusayn, Yaḥyā Ḥaqqī, Suhayl Idrīs and al-Ṭayyib Ṣāliḥ.[12] While al-Ṭahṭāwī's work certainly aroused

[10] Hourani, 84-94.
[11] Pantucek, 28.
[12] Jūrj Ṭarābīshī, *Sharq wa-gharb rujūla wa-unūtha*, Beirut: Dār al-Ṭalīʿa,

the interest of the Egyptian readership concerning European society and its bases, his importance within the early development of the novel lies more in the area of translation. He was placed in charge of a new School of Languages in 1836, and he and his pupils proceeded during the following decades to translate numerous significant works of European thought: Voltaire, Montesquieu, Fénélon, to name just a few.[13] To these were added, slowly but inevitably, works of literature. Among the first were the fables of La Fontaine and the novels of Alexandre Dumas. From the outset, therefore, the Egyptian readership was attuned to writings which had a generous dose of historical melodrama to them.

The avowed policy of westernisation espoused by the Khedive Ismāʿīl, who ruled from 1863 till 1879, may have been financially ruinous for the country, but it certainly provided a conducive environment in which this process of reacquaintance with European culture could take place. Above all, it appeared as a haven of safety and freedom of expression to the large number of Syrian Christians who came to Egypt following the civil war of the 1850s, bringing with them their expertise and research in the classical language and its literature, as well as early experiments in drama and numerous journals and magazines of both a scientific and cultural nature. Al-Ṭahṭāwī had, incidentally, also served as editor of the official Egyptian newspaper, *al-Waqāʾiʿ al-Miṣriyya*, but it was the infusion of new blood which led to a huge and rapid expansion of newspapers during the latter decades of the nineteenth century.

It is hard to overestimate the important role which the press has played in the revival of Arab cultural awareness during the last century.[14] It came to full fruition when nationalist sentiments and opposition to foreign domination were beginning to be heard; in fact, in many cases these causes led to the foundation of newspapers. However, in addition to providing a forum for the discussion of ideas concerning nationalism and Islamic reform, the newspapers and journals also published short stories, initially translations from European languages but gradually and inevitably including early experiments composed

1977; Issa J. Boullata, "Encounter between East and West: a theme in contemporary Arabic novels", *MEJ* XXX/1 (Winter 1976), 44-62.

[13] Hourani, 71.

[14] Vial, *EI*[2] art. "Ḳiṣṣa", sec. 2; Pantucek, 24.

in Arabic. There were even a few which were entirely devoted to the publication of such entertainment literature. The newspaper, *al-Ahrām*, for example, founded in Alexandria in 1875, provided a forum for a story and, indeed, still does. For this role of the press has not diminished with the increase in book publication; the Arab world's most famous novelist, Najīb Maḥfūẓ, continues to publish his works, of whatever length, for the first time in serial form. But even this should not cause any surprise, for, as R.G. Cox notes:

> ... a great deal of Victorian literature, verse and general prose as well as novels, was first published in periodicals; they can be seen as forming a vast nursery for its production ...

and later he adds that

> During the nineteenth century then, periodicals performed a wide variety of functions... They played a large part both in creating the public and in keeping it alive, active and at once receptive and critical ... At a more practical level the periodicals played an important part in furnishing an interim market for literary work.[15]

Novel writing is not a profession by which one can earn a living in the Arab world; not even Najīb Maḥfūẓ at the height of his fame has been able to devote himself entirely to writing. For that reason, the Arabic press has continued to play a valuable role in the development of the Arabic novel, firstly by making the works available to a wider public through serialisation, and secondly—in the case of the more well-known writers—by offering a variety of positions as editors in cultural journals and magazines, thus providing a regular source of income in an area not too far removed from their real sphere of interest. On the negative side, it has to be admitted that the abuse of this convenient employment opportunity has occasionally and, in some countries, often led to cronyism among the older generation of writers and to the virtual exclusion of younger generations from publication opportunities.

This brief survey of the circumstances surrounding the *nahḍa* in the different parts of the Arabic-speaking world has shown that, while the basic features were the same in each area, factors from history (the civil war in Syria of the 1850s, the policies of the colonial powers), geography, and politics (censorship, for

[15] Ch. in *From Dickens to Hardy. The Pelican guide to literature* VI, London: Pelican Books, 1958, 1960, 1963, 198, 202.

example)—to name just a few—combined to make the speed and chronology of the process quite different in the various countries under consideration. Within this frame of reference, the enlightened educational policies of Muḥammad ʿAlī, the influx of Syrian immigrants, the concentration of the British on matters of finance and administration rather than culture and education, and the geographic centrality of the country within the region, all these contributed to the emergence of Egypt as a major focal point of literary activity at the end of the nineteenth century and during the first decades of this century. It is the Iraqi writer, Jamīl Saʿīd, who comments:

> Iraqi writers did not produce much fiction because their colleagues in Egypt and Syria were ahead of them. Iraqi readers preferred to read books—on whatever subject—written by Egyptians rather than Iraqis; they even preferred books printed in Egypt rather than in Iraq.[16]

Thus, in dealing with the beginnings of the novelistic tradition in Arabic within the context of Egypt, we are talking chronologically about the earliest tradition, one which was a combination of two, those of Egypt and Syria-Lebanon. The development of the novel tradition moved along similar lines, *mutatis mutandis*, in the other regions of the Arabic-speaking world. And through that process of what Jabrā terms "rapid chain-explosions" and catching up on the "back-log", any such chronological differentials have by now been eliminated.[17]

The novels of Jurjī Zaydān are a splendid illustration of the Egyptian environment to which we have just referred. Zaydān (1861-1914) was a Lebanese immigrant to Egypt, where he founded in 1892 the magazine, *al-Hilāl*, which is still in existence. Like Faraḥ Anṭūn's *al-Jāmiʿa* and Yaʿqūb Ṣarrūf's *al-Muqtaṭaf*, Zaydān's journal was a major conduit for information on the history and science of the West. However, Zaydān was apparently also eager to acquaint his readership with aspects of the history of the Arabs and Islam (as a means of encouraging and fostering a new cultural awareness), while at the same time providing works of fiction which would entertain in the same way as some of the more melodramatic historical novels from Europe which had been serialised in the press. To this end, he

16 *Naẓarāt fī al-tayyārāt al-adabiyya al-ḥadītha fī al-ʿIrāq*, Cairo: Maʿhad al-dirāsāt al-ʿArabiyya al-ʿĀliyya, 1954, 7-8, also 25.

17 Jabrā, "Modern Arabic literature and the West", 81.

wrote a whole series of historical novels somewhat in the mode of Walter Scott.[18] A selection of titles, *Fatḥ al-Andalus* ("The conquest of Spain"), *al-Ḥajjāj ibn Yūsuf*, *Ṣalāḥ al-Dīn*, and *al-Inqilāb al-'Uthmānī* ("The Ottoman revolution"), makes it clear that Zaydān is pursuing his essentially pedagogical goals in writing these novels, but in each case the lesson of history is made more palatable through attention to local detail and, above all, by the provision of a love story. *Istibdād al-Mamālīk* "Mamlūk tyranny" is a typical example. Set in the time of 'Alī Bey al-Kabīr and his struggle with his son-in-law, Muḥammad Abū Dhahab (1769-73), the novel swings back and forth between Egypt and Syria (which the Egyptian army has invaded). The local colour is provided by the disasters which befall the family of Sayyid 'Abd al-Raḥmān, a wealthy merchant who finds himself prey to the exactions of the Mamlūks and who is forced to fight in the Egyptian army in order to save his son, Ḥasan, from a similar fate. Against the backdrop of the historical events leading to 'Alī Bey's defeat at the hands of Muḥammad Abū Dhahab, the family goes through a series of adventures, miraculous escapes from death, and disguises in order to emerge unscathed as Abū Dhahab celebrates his victory.

For all their combination of history and contrived romantic interest, not to mention the emphasis on action, these novels were far superior to many of the translated, adapted and original works which were being serialised during these decades, novels marked (rather like some contemporary Indian films) by a little bit of everything: murder, intrigue, love, fights, dancing and rapid action. The availability of such works did little to advance the development of the novel genre, and indeed appears to have given it something of a social stigma. Here one can draw an analogy with the theatrical tradition at this time in noting that the Egyptian intelligentsia did not regard the writings of such works with any favour, as will become clear when we consider shortly the case of Haykal. With these factors in mind, and considering the rapid development which the novel tradition has seen in this century, it is no small tribute to

[18] Sasson Somekh, *The changing rhythm*, Leiden: E.J. Brill, 1973, 7; 'Abd al-Muḥsin Ṭāhā Badr, *Taṭawwur al-riwāya al-'Arabiyya al-ḥadītha fī Miṣr*, Cairo: Dār al-Ma'ārif, 1963, 409-10. See now on Zaydān, Thomas Philipp, *Ǧurǧī Zaidān, his life and thought*, Beirut and Wiesbaden: Orient-Institut der DMG-Franz Steiner, 1979.

the pedagogical value and readability of Zaydān's novels that they are still available today.

While Zaydān culled his subject-matter from the past, other writers used the columns of the press to publish serialised works which commented on and criticised contemporary society and politics. Egypt in the 1890s provided a fertile subject for such scrutiny. Following the 'Urābī rebellion of 1882, with all the nationalist sentiments which it had aroused, the British had occupied the country, and Lord Cromer had been given the task of putting Egypt's finances in order. All this gave Muḥammad al-Muwayliḥī (1858-1930), an Egyptian journalist, plenty of material for his sarcastic pen. The resulting episodes, entitled *Fatra min al-zamān* ("A period of time"), were published over a four-year period (1898-1902) in the columns of his father's newspaper, *Miṣbāḥ al-Sharq*.[19] They were narrated by a young Egyptian named 'Īsā ibn Hishām, that being precisely the name used many centuries earlier by Badī' al-Zamān al-Hamadhānī in his *maqāmāt*. We are thus dealing with a conscious neo-classicism, something made abundantly clear at the beginning of each serialised episode which is composed of *saj'*, the rhyming prose style used in the *maqāmāt* genre which came to plague prose just as much as the excesses of *badī'* did poetry. With al-Muwayliḥī, however, this stylistic device is reserved for initial display, after which he moves into a clear and polished style reminiscent of the best classical models.[20]

The narrator meets a Turkish Pāshā from Muḥammad 'Alī's time who rises from the grave, and together they explore the many problems, inconsistencies, and ironies of life in Egypt some fifty years after the Pāshā's death, fifty years which have witnessed much modernisation and westernisation and, above all, the British occupation of the country. As this series of episodes evolved (and, as in some of the works of Dickens, that process can be seen as a response to the reaction of the readership), it was already being referred to as "The story of 'Īsā ibn Hishām". Thus, when al-Muwayliḥī decided to publish his serialised episodes as a book in 1907, it is hardly surprising that one of the first monuments of modern Arabic prose should

[19] Roger Allen, "Some new al-Muwailihi materials", *Humaniora Islamica* II (1974), 139-80.

[20] The work is studied at length in *idem*, *Al-Muwayliḥī's Ḥadīth 'Īsā ibn Hishām*, Albany: State University of New York Press, 1974.

have been given the title *Ḥadīth ʿĪsā ibn Hishām*. The work was an immediate success; a second edition appeared in 1912 and a third in 1923. In 1927 it was given some form of canonisation by being adopted as a school text, although, from my conversations with numerous Egyptians, that also seems to have secured the death of its popularity. This was also an unfortunate decision in that much of the more controversial (and therefore interesting) criticism of society which the first three editions had contained—pointed criticisms of al-Azhar, the Royal Family and Muḥammad ʿAlī's Turkish ways—was omitted, and in its place was inserted a number of episodes of *Fatra min al-zamān* describing a visit which ʿĪsā ibn Hishām (equals al-Muwayliḥī) made to the Great Exhibition in Paris in 1899. These episodes, now called *al-Riḥla al-thāniya*, may be yet another example of the "European visit" theme, but show none of the pungent sarcasm of the Egyptian episodes.

Several critics have tried to identify *Ḥadīth ʿĪsā ibn Hishām* as the beginning of the Egyptian novel, but there are a number of problems connected with such attempts. In the first place, if the work is to be considered a novel, then by any yardstick it is a thoroughly bad one. As is typical with a series of episodes written over a four-year period, the narrative thread is extremely contrived and often invisible. Only in certain chapters—the initial ones in which the Pāshā is heavily involved in the action, and the later ones involving that perennial figure of fun, the rustic *ʿumda*—is any real effort made to maintain continuity. Furthermore, there is no characterisation in any real sense of the word, and certainly no development of character through action. But all this is basically unfair to al-Muwayliḥī, since, in my opinion, he had no intention of writing a novel or the converting of his series of newspaper articles into one. That he did intend to produce a work of polished prose which would use aspects of a classical genre and style is not open to doubt, but the purpose of the work's publication was certainly more concerned with the politics of the day, as was appropriate for a journalist. Others, including the famous poet, Ḥāfiẓ Ibrāhīm, a close friend of al-Muwayliḥī, also wrote in the *maqāma* style while criticising the political situation in Egypt at the turn of the century, but these exercises in neo-classicism were to prove a dead end. They were overtaken by an increasing interest in European fictional genres. Thus *Ḥadīth ʿĪsā ibn Hishām* certainly demonstrated how a work of fiction could address itself forcibly to societal issues, but it must be considered a precursor to the novel genre in Arabic. It served a valuable role as a bridge between the forms and style of classical, or rather neo-classical, prose and the incipient novel tradition.

Muḥammad al-Muwayliḥī had used an extremely polished prose style in composing *Ḥadīth ʿĪsā ibn Hishām*, whereas Jurjī Zaydān in his series of historical novels had used a less lofty vehicle. In both cases the style reflects the attitudes and goals of the writer. The development of a modern Arabic prose style which could be adapted to these new genres obliges us to mention Muṣṭafā Luṭfī al-Manfalūṭī (1876-1924) who, once again through the medium of the press, published a whole series of essays and vignettes on a variety of topics; they appeared later in the form of two books, *al-Naẓarāt* and *al-ʿAbarāt*. The latter title ("Tears") demonstrates the excessively romantic and sentimental nature of the content of these works. From the first collection, *al-Ka's al-ūlā* ("The first glass") tells the story of a man who allows himself to drink a single glass of wine, whereupon his entire life disintegrates. Another piece, *Ṣidq wa-kidhb* ("Truth and falsehood") betrays in its title the way in which qualities are painted in terms of black and white, with few, if any, intermediate hues of grey. But to dwell on these faults is hardly necessary, since they were attacked with characteristic vigour by Ibrāhīm al-Māzinī in his famous critical work, *al-Dīwān*.[21] In any case, al-Manfalūṭī's works remain popular with adolescents to this day. What was significant about these essays was the way in which he conveyed his ideas, which were a curious mixture of Islamic modernism, an awareness of the classical heritage and anti-Western sentiments, a blend typical of the period at the turn of the century in which he wrote.[22] His style was straightforward, often in the form of a vignette, a letter which he had received, or an anecdote which he had heard. These "essays" introduced a new and captivating kind of literature to the Egyptian reading public, and that in a style which was immediately accessible. Thus while their content may place them firmly within the realm of early romanticism, their style provides an important step in the development of a crucial feature of the novel tradition.

21 ʿAbbās Maḥmūd al-ʿAqqād and Ibrāhīm al-Māzinī, *al-Dīwān*, Cairo, Nov. 1921, 1-32.

22 H.A.R. Gibb, *Studies on the civilization of Islam*, London: Routledge and Kegan Paul, 1962, 258-68.

Another unabashed romantic of the period was the Lebanese Khalīl Jubrān, who was to become the leader of the *mahjar* school in the United States. As in the case of al-Manfalūṭī, his fiction (which takes the form of short stories and some longer pieces) is extremely romantic, in Jubrān's case being written early in his career (1907-14). *Al-Ajniḥa al-mutakassira* ("Broken wings") and *al-Arwāḥ al-mutamarrida* ("Rebellious spirits") both show an extreme anti-clericalism (to which we referred earlier), while the fact that one of the figures in the latter work is "Khalīl the Heretic" points to the close personal involvement of the author in his characters.[23] Once again, it is all too easy to identify the unconvincing contrast between good and evil characters and phenomena. In the story "Martha from Bān" from the collection *'Arā'is al-murūj* ("Nymphs of the valley", thus the standard English translation, literally "of the fields"), for example, the contrast between the evil city and the good countryside is totally simplistic. The effect is accentuated in Jubrān's case by his disruptive authorial intrusions into the narrative in order to deliver homilies on moral and social issues.

All the works which we have discussed thus far contribute in one way or another to the emergence of the novel genre, be it in style, or in concern with social issues, or in aspects of technique. But none of these writers succeeded in placing real Arab characters into an authentic setting. This was the task of the would-be Arab novelist at this time, along with the need to overcome societal attitudes to the genre and to those who would write in it. Muḥammad Ḥusayn Haykal, resident in France in 1911 and nostalgic about his Egyptian homeland, undertook such a task.

Zaynab, considered by many critics to be the first non-historical Arabic novel, was published in Egypt in 1913 under the pseudonym *Misrī fallāḥ* ("A peasant-Egyptian") although, as Ḥamdī Sakkūt observes, the true identity of Haykal was known to literary critics at the time.[24] A primary feature of this work is the loving attention which is devoted to the description of the Egyptian countryside. If previous attempts at novel writing had lacked a realistic backdrop, then Haykal places his reader right in the midst of an Egyptian village, and proceeds to

23 Nadim Naimy, "The mind and thought of Khalil Gibran", *JAL* V (1974), 55-71.

24 *The Egyptian novel and its main trends 1913-1952*, Cairo: The American University in Cairo Press, 1971, 12.

elaborate on natural phenomena—the fields and crops, the sunrise and sunset, and so on—at great, almost tedious length. Not for nothing is the work subtitled *Manāẓir wa-akhlāq rīfiyya* ("Country scenes and manners"). One has to admit that the overall effect is more than a little sentimental, a fact attributable, no doubt, to the author's feelings of nostalgia while studying abroad. In fact, it is this feeling and the author's desire to make a clear statement about the status of women in Egyptian society which seems to have provided the major stimulus in the writing of the novel.

The plot is based on two focal points: Zaynab, a beautiful peasant girl who works in the fields owned by the father of the second focal point, Ḥāmid, a student in Cairo who returns to his parental home during the vacations and whose views seem very much a reflection of Haykal's own. The two foci meet briefly in that Zaynab is one of the girls with whom Ḥāmid flirts, but nothing comes of this dalliance, and their stories are essentially separate. To Ḥāmid, Zaynab serves as consolation when he learns that his cousin, ʿAzīza, with whom he has been carrying on some kind of epistolary love affair, is being married off to someone else. When he finally despairs of the prospect of finding true love, he goes back to Cairo and sends his parents a letter full of his ideas about society and its problems, ideas which are patently those of Haykal himself:

> Since the day I began thinking about love and happened to meet my cousin, I have wanted to marry her ... When I saw her and began to realise how impossible it was to find any opportunity to talk to her alone, I got very annoyed and became even more intolerant of society and its customs than those who have to put up with the painful tortures which it imposes on people. The subject of marriage became for me the object of the most bitter criticism ... In my opinion, marriage which is not based on love and which does not endure on the basis of love is despicable.[25]

This passage is an excellent illustration of the way in which societal moralising still intrudes into the narrative, although we have now made some limited progress from outright authorial homilies to the letter format. Furthermore, one can see all too clearly the problems of psychological fallacy here, as Ḥāmid the student in Cairo acquainted with Western works regarding liberty and justice, such as those of John Stuart Mill and

[25] Haykal, *Zaynab*, Cairo: Maktabat Nahḍat Miṣr, 1963, 268-9.

Herbert Spencer, proceeds to discuss the question of marriage in Egyptian society on such a lofty plane with his parents who have always lived deep in the Egyptian countryside.

Ḥāmid, however, does not lend his name to the title of this work, and we should now consider the other focus. Zaynab is also unable to marry the person whom she loves, in this case, Ibrāhīm, the poor fellow-worker who cannot afford the bride price. She therefore accedes to her parents' wish that she should marry Ḥasan, who can come up with the requisite amount. In spite of her love for Ibrāhīm, Zaynab does all she can to be a good wife to Ḥasan, who treats her most considerately. However, Ibrāhīm is so poor that he cannot even bribe his way out of military service as most other people seem to do, and as a result he is drafted into the army and sent off to fight in the Sudan. In what may be considered a classic version of the romantic ending, Zaynab begins to pine for her true beloved and dies of tuberculosis, asking with her dying breath that Ibrāhīm's handkerchief be buried with her. As we shall see in the next chapter, this is not the last time that such an ending is employed in the Arabic novel.

Within this narrative framework, both Zaynab and Ḥāmid emerge as victims of societal custom. Neither can marry the person whom he or she really loves. Furthermore, Ḥāmid's cousin, ʿAzīza, living in the city and apparently well-educated, seems, if anything, to have less freedom of movement than Zaynab herself who can walk around the village and fields unveiled and can even respond to Ḥāmid's advances. ʿAzīza does, of course, have the advantage of an education, but through Ḥāmid, Haykal is surely giving support to the ideas of the famous reformer, Qāsim Amīn, concerning women's rights. An implication of this novel is certainly that both Zaynab and ʿAzīza are victims of the same societal customs. Education can be of little use as long as they persist.[26] The portrayal of Zaynab dying with Ibrāhīm's handkerchief in her hand, and of Ḥāmid skulking in disillusionment in Cairo, are Haykal's symbols of the status of marriage in Egypt at the time when this novel was written.

During the course of this analysis, we have pointed out some of the obvious faults of this novel: the excessively descriptive

[26] Charles Smith, "Love, passion and class in the fiction of Muḥammad Ḥusayn Haykal", *JAOS* XCIX/2 (1979), 251.

passages, the flaws in characterisation and the somewhat saccharine sentimentality which clashes with the tastes of our own age, perhaps themselves excessively anti-romantic. However, this novel places genuine Egyptian people into an authentic local environment, and through its plot succeeds in airing some of the societal issues which the characters have to face. Furthermore, we have noted above that the characterisation is flawed, but from a historical viewpoint we should note that there *is* characterisation. To be sure, not all the people are portrayed with the same amount of detail, and the secondary characters are as two-dimensional as those of many previous novels; but the principal actors in this work do emerge as real people with emotions and beliefs which they project during the course of the narrative.

We have just used the term "actors", calling to mind the contribution of the dramatic aspect of the Aristotelian triad to the novel genre. As we noted earlier, the drama provides the element of dialogue, and it is here that Haykal broaches one of the most difficult problems in modern Arabic literature, that of the use of language. To digress somewhat, the term in Arabic for the written language is *al-fuṣḥā*, a word derived from the verbal base which means "to be eloquent" and "to use Arabic correctly". A further point which should be noticed is that the *form* of this word also implies an opinion: it is in the *ism al-tafḍīl* or "noun of superiority" form, thus giving the sense of "more eloquent" or "more correct". The colloquial dialect is by contrast given the term *ʿāmmiyya*, and the attitude of the literary establishment to it is well captured in the words of Ṭāhā Ḥusayn, the great Egyptian littérateur (1889-1973), in his work *Mustaqbal al-thaqāfa fī Miṣr* ("The future of culture in Egypt"):

I am now and will always remain unalterably opposed to those who regard the colloquial as a suitable instrument for mutual understanding and a method for realising the various goals of our intellectual life ... The colloquial lacks the qualities to make it worthy of the name of a language. I look on it as a dialect that has been corrupted in many respects. It might disappear, as it were, into the classical if we devoted the necessary effort on the one hand to elevate the cultural level of the people and on the other to simplify and reform the classical so that the two meet at a common point.[27]

[27] *The future of culture in Egypt*, trans. Sidney Glazer, Washington: American Council of Learned Societies, 1954, 86.

Discussion of this issue has raged fiercely during most of the first half of this century, and with most vigour, needless to say, within the realm of the theatre. In the novel form, the writer's communication with the recipient is neither visual nor aural, but the question of the use of the colloquial language in dialogue in the fictional genres has been fought out with great intensity. The majority of creative writers have in fact done exactly as they saw fit, leaving the polemics to critics. Nevertheless, as the novel has developed, each writer has had to make a conscious decision as to which language to use in his works and, if he becomes famous, to justify his choice. As we consider the Arabic novel in its initial phases, it is therefore interesting to note that Haykal uses the colloquial language in his dialogue, although we have also to admit that there is not a great deal of it in this novel, one packed so full of description.

Haykal's work was noted and reviewed at the time of its appearance, but it did not stimulate an increased interest in the novel genre. ʿAbd al-Muḥsin Ṭāhā Badr shows in his important work on the development of the modern Arabic novel in Egypt until 1938 that novels were being written both before and after 1913, but that they tended to belong to the entertainment, melodramatic category which has been alluded to above rather than to a developing literary tradition.[28] *Zaynab* was published in a second edition, but not until 1929, by which time Haykal was well-known both as editor of a famous newspaper and as a cultural figure of some renown. The republication of the work and the discussion which surrounded it stimulated a tremendous interest in the genre which was to bear fruit in the next decade.[29] But in the intervening years, much had been happening in the realm of prose literature. In the first place, these years saw the rise to prominence of the short story genre. At the hands of Muḥammad Taymūr the form still shows signs of the didactic purpose evident in the earlier examples of Jubrān and al-Manfalūṭī. In the story *Fī al-qiṭār* ("In the train"), for example, the topic of public education is discussed in a train compartment by a group of stereotypical Egyptian characters within a situation, the beginning and end of which are very contrived. However, once again an effort is being made to use real characters or at least types in order to reflect the problems of the

[28] *Taṭawwur al-riwāya*, 411-21.

[29] Gibb, *op. cit.*, 294-8.

society in which they live. The early efforts of Taymūr were continued in the 1920s by his brother, Maḥmūd (born 1894) who has since then written an enormous number of short stories, several of the later ones involving revisions of earlier works which show a developing awareness of technique.[30] Maḥmūd Taymūr, along with Maḥmūd Ṭāhir Lāshīn, Yaḥyā Ḥaqqī and others, instituted a movement of young writers who called themselves *al-Madrasa al-ḥadītha* ("The new school"), a group about which Ḥaqqī writes with much affection in his important study, *Fajr al-qiṣṣa al-Miṣriyya*.[31] They were much influenced by the writing of European short story writers, particularly de Maupassant, and Russians such as Turgenev, Chekov and Dostoevsky. This influence is immediately apparent in the first stories of Maḥmūd Taymūr, which began to appear in profusion in 1925. The very titles, *Shaykh Jum'a* and *Shaykh Sayyid al-'Abīṭ*, *al-Ḥājj Shalabī* and *'Amm Mitwallī*, show them to be what they are, vignettes which depict, in the economic and yet vivid detail required in a short story, the ordinary lives and customs of Egyptians. The importance of the success and popularity of these stories lies not only in the impetus which it gave to the writers of this "New school" and others to continue writing in the shorter genre, but also because it gave a clear indication to would-be novelists of the way in which skilful character portrayal could be used to good effect within the novel format.

Another major contribution to prose literature during this decade was one of the most beloved of all works in modern Arabic literature, *al-Ayyām*, Tāhā Husayn's famous autobiography, originally serialised in *al-Hilāl* and then published as a book. Almost every commentator on the modern Arabic novel includes some reference to this work, and rightly so. The fact that it is written in the third person lends an element of fictionality even to these personal memories, and this is aided by both the insights into the young boy's motivations and also by the tone of gentle irony which pervades the entire work. When we couple with these qualities a limpid prose style which flows with such deceptive ease, the sum total is a work which has

[30] Mattityahu Peled, *al-Uqṣūṣa al-Taymūriyya fī marḥalatayni*, Tel Aviv: Tel Aviv University, 1977.

[31] Cairo: al-Hay'a al-Miṣriyya al-'Āmma, 1975, 75-98.

remained one of the most enduring masterpieces in all of modern Arabic prose literature.

These, then, are some of the factors which helped to stimulate an increased interest in the novel genre, so much so that in the 1930s a large number of littérateurs seem to have felt themselves almost constrained to write a novel; as though, after being an object of societal opprobium a few decades earlier, it had now become something of a vogue. The publication of the second edition of Haykal's work seems to have prompted particular interest, in that a competition in novel writing was announced in the following year. The eventual winner was *Ibrāhīm al-kātib* ("Ibrāhīm the author", 1931) by Ibrāhīm al-Māzinī.[32]

The title of this work suggests a feature which is especially prominent in the series of novels written by Egyptians in this decade, namely their autobiographical nature (to a greater or lesser degree). While al-Māzinī himself consistently denied it, most critics agree that "Ibrāhīm the author" is precisely that. The story itself is a rather disjointed account of the love of a man for three different women: a Syrian nurse, Mary, who helps him through his convalescence from illness; his cousin, Shūshū; and Laylā, a girl whom he meets in Luxor where he has gone to escape from the memory of his failure to marry Shūshū. In this work as in Haykal's, there is implicit criticism of societal customs, in that Ibrāhīm is not allowed to marry Shūshū whom he loves because her elder sister is still unmarried. There is an inconsistency in al-Māzinī's treatment of this theme, in that Shūshū eventually is married to a doctor even though her elder sister remains unmarried. However, we have suggested above that a clear narrative thread is not the major virtue of this novel. Where it does represent an advance is in characterisation. As is evident from al-Māzinī's short stories, he is a master in pen-portraits of characters and types, particularly when he has the opportunity to pepper the sketch with some of his unique brand of humour. Many situations in the work—the narrator's experiences with Aḥmad al-Mayyit (meaning "the dead") at his cousins' house, the strange encounter with the man who has robbed him in Alexandria, to list just two—illustrate that same, almost farcical sense of fun which typifies so many of his stories. Thus if this work it not entirely successful, it still provides the

[32] *Ibrahim the writer*, trans. Magdi Wahba, Cairo: General Egyptian Book Organization, 1976.

reader with some memorable Egyptian characters and some poignant and amusing moments.

It is no accident that the first novel which succeeded in giving a totally convincing portrait of a family within a very restricted environment should have been written by Tawfīq al-Ḥakīm, whose major interest has been and remains the drama. In *'Awdat al-rūḥ* ("Return of the spirit", 1933) we are introduced to Muḥsin, a young student living with his relatives in Cairo. Through a dialogue of considerable subtlety and variety, we are introduced to the various members of the closely-knit family; the male members all find themselves fascinated by the charm of the daughter of a neighbour, Saniyya, while in contrast Zannūba, the spinster of the family, spends large amounts of money on beautifying herself in an attempt to find a husband. The promising nature of this situation is however spoiled when, in the central part of the work, Muḥsin returns to his parent's country estate for the vacation. This allows al-Ḥakīm to elaborate on the theme which provides the novel with its title: the Pharaonism movement which had a considerable vogue at the time when this work was written, sc. the idea of eternal Egypt, unchanging in spite of the passage of time and the succession of foreign occupiers. The application of this idea to the 1919 Revolution in Egypt, in which the members of the family are finally involved, may be appropriate in itself, but the attempt to combine this heavily symbolic motif with the lively and realistic portrait which forms the first part of the work is a failure, and the work loses its sense of balance. Once again, one facet of the complex process of novel writing has been convincingly demonstrated in paving the way for the emergence of the Arabic novel in its full maturity.

A second work, *'Uṣfūr min al-sharq* ("Bird from the East", 1938) takes the student, Muḥsin, to Paris in order to continue his studies, suggesting again an autobiographical link between character and author. The work is used to suggest a rather facile contrast between the spiritual East and the material West in a way which shows little characterisation or action and which can be seen as an early precedent to the more sophisticated treatment of the same "Arab student in Europe" theme to be found in later works by Yaḥyā Ḥaqqī, Suhayl Idrīs and al-Ṭayyib Ṣāliḥ to which we shall refer later. The same subject is to be found in Ṭāhā Ḥusayn's *Adīb* (1935), but once again the subject of European education is allowed to preponderate. That topic, together with the excessive use of the letter format, produces a rather tedious work. Ṭāhā Ḥusayn's later novels, and particularly *Shajarat al-bu's* ("Tree of misery", 1944), are much more successful contributions to the genre.

In yet another novel from this decade, Tawfīq al-Ḥakīm succeeded in creating one of the most memorable works of early modern Arabic fiction, *Yawmiyyāt nā'ib fī al-aryāf* ("Diary of a prosecutor in the provinces", 1937).[33] Once again, this work obviously owes a great deal to the author's own experiences as a prosecutor. His first hand knowledge enables him to give a moving, amusing, and forceful portrait of the Egyptian peasantry trying to pursue their lives according to time-honoured customs, while bureaucracy and the judiciary find myriad ways of preventing them from doing so. This brilliant exposé of the foibles of a literalist establishment rightly remains popular to the present day.

Another contributor to this process was the poet and critic, ʿAbbās Maḥmūd al-ʿAqqād, with *Sāra* (1938).[34] Al-ʿAqqād was to a large degree self-taught, and combined interests in literature with those in the natural sciences. It is thus perhaps hardly surprising that he became involved in the use of psychological analysis as it could be applied to literature, as, for example, in his study of the famous classical poet Ibn al-Rūmī.[35] His contribution to the novel certainly falls within this category, and, in his Introduction to the second edition, he himself suggests that *Sāra* is either "a novel of psychological analysis or an analysis in a narrative form".[36] The analysis concerns the breakdown of a love affair between Hammām and Sāra, and the author's technique becomes clear from the titles of individual chapters, many of which take the form of questions: "Who was she?", "How did he get to know her?", "Why did he fall in love with her?". There is almost no background against which this detailed dissection is conducted, and very little action or dialogue to provide some relief from the relentless process of investigation. The psychological dimension may be explored in

33 *The maze of justice*, trans. A.S. Eban, London: The Harvill Press, 1947.

34 *Sara*, trans. Muṣṭafā Badawī, Cairo: General Egyptian Book Organization, 1978.

35 See *Ibn al-Rūmī: ḥayātuhu min shiʿrihi*, Cairo: Maṭbaʿat Ḥijāzī, 1938; David Semah, *Four Egyptian literary critics*, Leiden: E.J. Brill, 1974, 3-65.

36 *Sara*, trans. Mustafa Badawi, Introduction, 12.

depth, and indeed later writers may have benefited from this example, but the overall effect is extremely tedious.

Ṭāhā Ḥusayn, al-ʿAqqād and al-Ḥakīm are three of the most illustrious names in the history of modern Arabic literature, and it is a sign of the increasing interest in the novel genre that they wrote the works which we have just described. However, alongside the developing skills which are evident in these works are obvious flaws in technique. With that in mind, it is both sad and ironic that a novel written during this decade which *does* show a considerable artistic consistency, Maḥmūd Ṭāhir Lāshīn's *Ḥawwā' bilā Ādam* ("Eve without Adam", 1934), has suffered from the same neglect which has affected the author's work as a whole and which seems to have contributed in no small way to his decision to stop writing. What makes this work particularly noteworthy is not only that it seems to be a piece of complete fiction—in other words, without any autobiographical content or allusions—but also that "the outcome appears as a natural development from the interaction of characters and their environment".[37] Through the character of Ḥawwā', an orphaned girl who has been brought up by her grandmother and who works as a teacher, Lāshīn provides his readers with an effective illustration of the incompatibility between the dicta of modern education (particularly with regard to the emancipation of women) and traditional values. Ḥawwā' herself is well educated and belongs to a feminist society, before which she delivers a stirring speech on education and its goals. However, her lonely and cloistered upbringing has not provided her with any experience on emotional matters, but has rather stifled them. Thus when she falls in love with the brother of the aristocratic girl whom she is tutoring, a young man considerably younger than herself, her feelings run away with her, if only in her own mind. When the young man is engaged to another girl, Ḥawwā''s entire life collapses. After agreeing to her grandmother's suggestion that they use magic and exorcism—the very personification of the values which she has been rejecting—she commits suicide.

This novel addresses itself forcibly to some prominent societal issues, and the statements and actions of the characters contribute to the discussion in a realistic and logical fashion. It

[37] Hilary Kilpatrick, *The modern Egyptian novel*, London: Ithaca Press, 1974, 51.

succeeds to a remarkable degree in combining several of the different facets in novel composition into a satisfactory unity, all of which makes one regret that the next generation of writers was apparently unaware of his achievement. Lāshīn himself chose to spend the rest of his working life in the Department of Public Works. In the words of Hilary Kilpatrick, "his silence was Egypt's loss".

* * *

Egypt was chosen to provide a model for the development of a novelistic tradition in the Arabic-speaking world, it will be recalled, because historical, geographical and cultural factors combined to make it the most chronologically-advanced milieu during the period which we have been considering. In other parts of the region analogous processes were occurring; the chronology and local features were, needless to say, varied, but the basic sequence was the same: firstly, translation and/or arabisation; secondly, imitation or adaptation; and then indigenous creation.

The most prominent prose writers in the Syro-Lebanese tradition up till the beginning of the Second World War were the members of the *mahjar* school in the United States. We have already mentioned the works of Khalīl Jubrān, but more sophisticated by far were the writings of his friend and biographer, Mīkhā'īl Na'īma, who returned to his native Lebanon one year after Jubrān's death in 1932. Like al-Māzinī and al-'Aqqād, Na'īma combined the talents of prose writer, poet, and critic, and indeed his collection of critical essays, *al-Ghurbāl* ("The sieve", 1923) is a major monument in modern Arabic literary criticism. Some episodes of his first novel, *Mudhakkirāt al-arqash* ("Memoirs of the man with the pitted face", 1949) were published as early as 1917, but his other novels belong to the period following the Second World War. More significant at this early stage were his short stories, many of which are set in Lebanon. In this case, however, we are not dealing with the simplistic contrasts of Jubrān (which Na'īma himself commented on negatively in his biography), but with brief sketches of characters and events which illustrate the beliefs of Lebanese people and particularly those of the mountain villages, and their attitudes to their families, to their neighbours and to new ideas. Titles such as *Sanatuhā al-jadīda* ("Her New Year") and *Maṣra' Sattūt* ("Sattūt's demise") are masterly portraits of the entrenched attitudes concerning family life, children, and the like, while *al-Bankārūliyā* ("The Bancarolia") is a suitably sardonic treatment of the response of a mountain family to the lures of the West and especially its education when it succeeds in consuming their entire worldly income. One of Naʿīma's most memorable portraits is that of "Abū Baṭṭa", an aged porter used to carrying the heaviest loads; he is finally asked to carry a load of barrels which is just too heavy (for him or anyone else) and at the conclusion of the story totters to the ground dead as the barrels roll over him. Naʿīma's variegated career, spanning two continents and many decades, serves as an excellent base for the further development of the fictional genres in his homeland.[38]

As Yūsuf ʿIzz al-Dīn demonstrates in his study of the development of the novel in Iraq, many features present there were similar to those in Egypt. The beginnings of prose fiction were again tied closely to the emergence of a press tradition, something which Ottoman censorship kept under tighter control. Initial experiments in novel writing tend to fall into the historical and/or entertainment categories, including within the former category a translated historical novel about King Henry the Fourth of England entitled *al-ʿAdl asās al-mulk* ("Justice is the basis of monarchy", 1909) and another by Sulaymān al-Dakhīl entitled *Nāẓim Pāshā* (1911), which claims to be a literary historico-socio-political story.[39] Similar to al-Muwayliḥī's often sarcastic approach to social reform is Sulaymān Fayḍī's *al-Riwāya al-īqāẓiyya* (1919). At the beginning of the work there is a rather facile comparison between Khiḍr, a poor boy who is going to school, and Bāqil, the son of a rich merchant who reflects his father's belief that education is a waste of time. In time, however, Bāqil is persuaded by his poorer friend to go to school and changes his name to Saʿīd.

[38] Mikhail Naimy, *A new year*, trans. John Perry, Leiden: E.J. Brill, 1974; C. Nijland, *Mīkhāʾīl Nuʿaymah, promotor of the Arabic literary revival*, Istanbul: Nederlands Historisch-Archaeologisch Instituut te Istanbul, 1975. Several Lebanese scholars have informed me that, in spite of many writings to the contrary, the name of this author is "Naʿīma" and not "Nuʿayma" (the diminutive form). Hence the insistence of him and his family on using the spelling "Naimy" (with the Lebanese "y" substituting for "a") in all English-language contexts.

[39] Yūsuf ʿIzz al-Dīn, *al-Riwāya fī al-ʿIrāq*, Cairo: Maʿhad al-Dirāsāt al-ʿArabiyya al-ʿĀliya, 1973, 18-20.

Under this new name, his studies proceed apace and he goes to France to study medicine at the Sorbonne while Khiḍr completes a degree in industrial engineering. The remainder of the work is concerned with Sa'īd's battles with his father and the generation which he represents over such matters as marriage, education, and health. At this early stage in the development of a fictional tradition in Iraq there is the almost inevitable homiletic and didactic tone to much of the work and especially this latter part. However, like al-Muwayliḥī's work in Egypt, Fayḍī's is an interesting initial essay in the application of fiction to social issues, although the flaws in technique are clear enough.

Further developments in the Iraqi fictional tradition during the period before 1939 were to take place primarily in the short story genre. The most famous prose writer of the period was Maḥmūd Aḥmad al-Sayyid. His novel, *Fī sabīl al-zawāj* ("On the path of marriage," 1921), is a highly romantic and melodramatic tale set in India, a country which al-Sayyid had visited during the course of the British occupation of Iraq following the First World War and the Iraqi Revolt which followed in 1920. While there is a certain amount of implicit criticism of the position of women in society within this work, it remains very much in the swashbuckling tradition of much European historical fiction and has not a little of the flavour of the *Thousand and one nights* as well. The contribution of both al-Sayyid and his contemporary, Anwar Shā'ūl, to the short story were of more lasting impact on Iraqi fiction than this rather cinematic work.[40]

"The development of the Arabic novel in the Maghrib", says Muḥammad 'Afīfī in his study of the Maghribi novel and drama, "was influenced to a large degree stylistically, artistically and creatively by the development of the literary press, by Western genre definitions, and by examples of Western works which were translated in the press".[41] Here, too, the influence of al-Muwayliḥī is very evident, although once again at a later stage. In the 1920s, Muḥammad 'Abdallāh al-Mu'aqqit wrote his *al-Riḥla al-Marrākushiyya* in which a narrator uses a Shaykh 'Abd al-Hādī to guide him on his travels to and around the Maghrib. However, while such stylistic and thematic pastiches

40 *Ibid.*, 65-75; Jamīl Sa'īd, *Naẓarāt fī al-tayyārāt al-adabiyya*, 7-24.

41 *al-Fann al-qaṣaṣī wa-al-masraḥī fī al-Maghrib al-'Arabī 1900-1965*, n.p.: Dār al-Fikr, 1971, 85-6.

seem to have been possible in the cultural environment of the countries of the Maghrib earlier in this century, the general conservatism of the system of Islamic education and the increasing prevalence of French as the language of higher culture combined to retard the development of a narrative prose tradition in Arabic till comparatively recently. Pantucek can describe the situation in Algeria by saying that "il serait difficile de qualifier cette période de véritable expansion au sens propre des belles-lettres".[42] Muḥammad ʿAfīfī expresses the opinion in 1961 that "the narrative art in Morocco is still in the formative stage; it has yet to achieve a personality of its own, and, if any well-integrated works exist, they are very few in number".[43]

The countries of the larger Maghrib have embarked on programmes of arabising their culture and of affording more opportunities for the publication of works of belles-lettres in Arabic. The period during which these efforts have been under way varies from one country to another, but they are already bearing fruit. It seems inevitable that the sophisticated belles-lettrist tradition in French within these countries which has already contributed many notable works to the novel tradition in French will continue to provide influence and support for the developing Arabic novel tradition in the region.

* * *

Hilary Kilpatrick begins an article, "The Arabic novel—a single tradition?", with an alarming, yet pertinent, question: "Does the Arabic novel exist?".[44] While acknowledging that, in comparison with Egypt, the novel was slow to develop in the other countries of the Arab world, she points out that the process of the *nahḍa*, characterised (as in any such movement) by occasional false starts and accelerations, has now done its own chronological levelling. The tradition of the Arabic novel has progressed in both maturity and originality since the Second World War, and today constitutes a vigorous cultural medium based on common factors of language, cultural and religious heritage, and on the effects of a response to recent colonial occupation. Within this larger framework, it is also true—and

[42] *Op. cit.*, 81-2.

[43] *al-Qiṣṣa al-Maghribiyya al-ḥadītha*, Casablanca: Maktabat al-Waḥda al-ʿArabiyya, 1961, 7.

[44] *JAL* V (1974), 93-107.

undoubtedly desirable—that there are a number of local traditions, each one reflecting the political, social, and cultural priorities and biases of the region. It is this happy mixture of unity and diversity which will be studied in the next chapter.

CHAPTER III

THE PERIOD OF MATURITY

1. *Introduction*

The novel, according to Philippe Sollers, is "la manière dont cette societé se parle".[1] During the last four decades the societies within the Arab world have witnessed changes on a wide scale in both their political and economic way of life. It should come as no surprise therefore that this same period has seen a tremendous expansion within the field of the Arabic novel. It is the purpose of this chapter to trace the developments and experiments which have taken place by examining themes and techniques used by novelists writing since the outset of the Second World War. However, bearing in mind the close connection noted above between novel writing and circumstances within society (however "pure" some writers and critics may wish the genre to be[2]), it seems useful to give a brief summary of some of the major events and trends in the Arab world against the background of which this outpouring of fiction will be viewed.

To the West the mention of the Arab world has traditionally invoked images of the camel and the *kaffiyya* with its headband. To these stereotypes has surely been added that of the oil well in recent decades. The discovery of oil in the Arab world has of course had an immense impact on the recent history of the region and has caused a radical shift in the balance of influence within the area itself and of economic power within the world as a whole. ʿAbd al-Raḥmān Munīf, whose novel *al-Nihāyāt* ("Endings", 1978) will be examined in detail in the next chapter, asserts in an interview that

> ... oil as a world and a topic may help uncover some novelistic aspects in our contemporary life in the Arab world.[3]

It has to be admitted that he is a petroleum economist by profession, and thus may be not a little *parti pris*; incidentally,

[1] Quoted in Jonathan Culler, *Structuralist poetics*, Ithaca, New York: Cornell University Press, 1975, 189.

[2] See Booth, *The rhetoric of fiction*, part 1, ch. IV, 89 ff.

[3] *al-Maʿrifa* 204 (Feb. 1979), 188.

we will be examining later what has been the effect of novel-writing as an avocation on the development of the genre in the Arab world. In his recent work, *al-Baḥth ʿan Walīd Masʿūd* ("In search of Walīd Masʿūd", 1978), Jabrā Ibrāhīm Jabrā provides us with a historical frame of reference on this point from which to view the extent of the changes which have occurred. Ibrāhīm al-Ḥājj Nawfal, one of the narrators in the novel, comments on his career as a businessman in Iraq and points out to his audience that he had been writing about economics at a time when

> the demand that Iraq have a twenty-per cent share in the revenues of the British Petroleum Company was regarded as a nationalist demand which would prove enormously difficult to achieve and would require both perseverance and determination.[4]

To a world now accustomed to awaiting each meeting of the OPEC nations with a combination of bated breath and resignation the shift in economic balance is surely striking.

These current realities are part of the larger and longer process, namely the complex web of relationships between the cultures of East and West, itself the subject of a whole series of novels. A comparison of al-Ṭayyib Ṣāliḥ's novel, *Mawsim al-hijra ilā al-shamāl* ("Season of migration to the North", 1969)—discussed in the next chapter—with earlier works in which Arabs give their impressions of Europe and Europeans provides another illustration of the changing nature of the relationship between the cultures (which Ṣāliḥ terms North and South).

In an earlier chapter we described the process whereby the Arab world "rediscovered" Europe during the nineteenth century. The interest of Europe in the Arab world took a rather more pragmatic form as France and Britain occupied, or otherwise participated in the governmental process of, various countries in the region. A natural reaction to this was the formation of a number of nationalist movements whose aspirations, whether purely local or pan-Arab, were dashed by the mandate agreements which followed the First World War. It is not insignificant that the year 1919 saw a popular revolution in Egypt, one which is still used by littérateurs in all genres as a symbol of resistance to foreign domination in any form and of the expression of the popular will. During the interwar period, much energy was focused on the writing of treatises on

[4] *al-Baḥth ʿan Walīd Masʿūd*, Beirut: Dār al-Ādāb, 1978, 311.

nationalism, involving such famous figures as Qusṭanṭīn Zurayq, Edmond Rabbāth and Sāṭiʿ al-Ḥuṣrī (whose writings, as Hourani notes, were published at a later date because "an active career left little time for systematic writing"[5]). In the case of Egypt, this tended to be a period of concentration on local nationalism, and the process did produce a certain limited progress towards independence through treaties with Britain. However, when the dogs of the Second World War proceeded to bark their noisy and disruptive way across the region, any forward momentum in the direction of independence was postponed. Britain's presence in Egypt during the war years is well captured for us in Najīb Maḥfūẓ's famous novel, *Zuqāq al-Midaqq* ("Midaqq Alley", 1947[6]).

The Second World War and its consequences brought about a change in the patterns of Western influence and hegemony in the Middle East. Furthermore, the efforts of nationalists in various countries to establish a theoretical and practical base now seemed on the point of bearing fruit. The Arab League was founded in Cairo in 1945. Much of the earlier agitation for Arab nationalism had been brought about by Syrian, Iraqi and Lebanese intellectuals, but the impact of the war on Egypt in general and on its political life in particular had no doubt made Egyptian politicians and intellectuals aware of the changing circumstances which the war would bring about and of the advantages of a united front. The choice of the Egyptian capital as the site for the League's headquarters not only acknowledged Cairo's central geographical position in the Arab world but also symbolised a role for Egypt which ʿAbd al-Nāṣir was to pursue with vigour in the next decade.

Hisham Sharabi is of the opinion, in retrospect, that from the outset "the League fell far short of the hopes and aspirations of most Arab Nationalists".[7] In any case, the newly-created body was presented within a year or so with a major crisis, one which again involved the Western Powers, namely the establishment of the state of Israel. The period which we are considering in this chapter is punctuated with unfortunate regularity by

[5] *Arabic thought in the liberal age*, 312.

[6] Translated by Trevor le Gassick as *Midaq Alley*, Beirut: Khayat, 1966; reprinted in London: Heinemann, and Washington: Three Continents Press, 1974.

[7] *Nationalism and revolution in the Arab world*, Princeton: Van Nostrand Co., 1966, 8.

conflict between the Arabs and the Zionist state. The years 1948, 1956 and 1967 (and, some would add, 1973 which Berque terms a "semi-success"[8]) are important events in the history of the modern Arab world, and their relative significance can be gauged—at least in part—by the treatment which they have received at the hands of Arab novelists, a subject to which we will return below.

The fighting in 1948 over the establishment of Israel was just one in a whole series of events in the decade following the Second World War which Berque has rightly termed "a decisive juncture in contemporary Arab history":

> The assassination of an Egyptian prime minister bore witness to the rise of extremism, the founding of the Baʿth party and the "free officers" conspiracy signaled the summons to new political horizons."[9]

The 1950s witnessed a number of revolutions in the Arab world (1952 in Egypt, for example, and 1958 in Iraq and the Sudan). There was also prolonged fighting in Algeria, leading to eventual independence in 1962. There were attempts at union: one which was implemented between Egypt and Syria—the United Arab Republic, 1958-61; and another attempt to include Iraq in the Republic which was never brought to full fruition. The arms deal with the Czechs in 1955, the withdrawal of the British and French from Suez and the nationalisation of the Suez Canal, the beginnings of the movement of non-aligned nations; these were heady days indeed. With all this movement and sense of dynamism, it is hardly surprising that this was also a period of intense discussion of the role of literature and the writer in society.[10] The decade of the 1950s saw an intense argument over the issue of commitment. The foundation of the literary periodical *al-Ādāb* in 1953 was and has remained the most obvious symbol of the development in these decades of a movement whose bases are well summarised in the quotation from Ra'īf al-Khūrī to the effect that

> The Arab writer is committed, particularly in this period of Arab

[8] *Cultural expression in Arab society today*, 93.

[9] *Ibid.*, 271.

[10] That the coincidence of these political and literary phenomena is in fact no accident is suggested by Berque, *op. cit.*, 271, and Mustafa Badawi, *A critical introduction to modern Arabic poetry*, Cambridge: Cambridge University Press, 1975, 207-8.

national revival, to producing works with a conscious and deliberate political meaning.[11]

As will be shown below, the novel, "as the model by which society conceives of itself, the discourse in and through which it articulates the world",[12] has been one of the primary areas of such activity and of critical commentary on it.

And yet, amid all the dynamism there were also profound doubts about the direction in which the Arab world was heading and the means which were being used to get it there. Littérateurs were not slow to express their views along these lines, often at considerable cost to their own well-being. Poems were written which expressed varying degrees of dissatisfaction and disgust with the state of Arab society; one thinks of Qabbānī's *Khubz wa-ḥashīsh wa-qamar* ("Bread, hashish and moonlight", 1955), Adūnīs's *Marthiyat al-ayyām al-ḥāḍira*, ("Elegy for the Present Days", 1958) and Ḥāwī's *al-ʿĀzar ʿām 1962* ("Lazarus 1962", 1965). In the same recent novel from which we quoted earlier, Jabrā once again provides us with a clear expression of views on this subject. Parenthetically, I might point out that Jabrā's predilection for setting the action of his novels among groups of intellectuals and his use of the multi-narrator technique serve to make his novels a goldmine of views on a whole variety of subjects connected with life in the modern Arab world. In the current instance, we are dealing with the main character of this novel, Walīd Masʿūd, the Palestinian who emerges from a period in an Israeli prison during which he has been tortured. In an unforgettable passage he describes the darker side of Arab society at this time:

> I saw my homeland for which I had just been prepared to go through the very tortures of Hell itself applying those very same tortures to anyone who fell into the hands of the people in authority. From the Arab Gulf to the Atlantic Ocean I heard a cry, I heard weeping and the sound of sticks and plastic hoses. Capitals and casbas, the secret police were everywhere, on mountain tops and in the valleys below; men in neat civilian suits walking to and fro like a thousand shuttles on a thousand looms, hauling off to the centres of darkness people by the tens and hundreds ...[13]

The almost sneering use of ʿAbd al-Nāṣir's ringing phrase of

11 See al-Jayyusi, *Trends and movements in modern Arabic poetry*, 575.

12 Culler, *Structuralist poetics*, 189.

13 *al-Baḥth ʿan Walīd Masʿūd*, 249.

Arab unity, "from the Arab Gulf to the Atlantic Ocean", draws attention to the grim side of life in Egypt in the 1960s which has been illustrated in considerable detail in Najīb Maḥfūẓ's *al-Karnak* (1974).[14] And that the situation is not unique to Egypt will be seen below when we consider in the next chapter the quartet of novels by the Iraqi writer Ismā'īl Fahd Ismā'īl.

The 1960s emerge then as a decade when the different revolutionary régimes in the Arab world moved from the initial flush of success which independence and its aftermath had brought towards a process of formulating some of the ideological principles on which the revolution had been or was to be based and of putting such principles into practice. This process almost inevitably led to a number of challenges, particularly from those whose view of revolution in general and of the particular revolution in question was different from that of the authorities. The challenges which took written form were of varying degrees of frankness. The copious use of symbolism at this time, as many novelists have observed, was not merely an artistic phenomenon but a matter of strict practicality. The more explicit writers could be handled with considerable severity, as Sabri Hafez notes.[15] The attitude of intellectuals to the governmental structure in Egypt and their alienation is portrayed with brilliant clarity in Maḥfūẓ's novel, *Tharthara fawq al-Nīl* ("Chatter on the Nile", 1966) which will be analysed in detail in the following chapter.

And then came the devastating June War of 1967. As Ḥalīm Barakāt illustrates so well in his novel, *'Awdat al-ṭā'ir ilā al-baḥr* ("The return of the Flying Dutchman to the sea", 1969), this was a war without heroes for the Arabs. As far as the air battle was concerned—and that was crucial—it was all over much too quickly. What made the impact even worse and the anger more intense was that the Arab world was being told by its leaders until the very last moment that it was on its way to a glorious victory. In the view of many, these events provided an all-too-graphic illustration of the kinds of problems to which intellectuals had been addressing themselves; but now the extent of the disease was shown to be so great that there was no longer a

[14] See also Raymond William Baker, *Egypt's uncertain revolution under Nasser and Sadat*, Cambridge, Mass.: Harvard University Press, 1978, 151.

[15] "The Egyptian novel in the sixties", *JAL* VII (1976), esp. 77. See also Yūsuf Idrīs, as quoted in the *New York Times Review of Books*, 16 March 1980, 3 ff.

question of suppressing overt discussion of its many ramifications. What ensued has been characterised by Abdallah Laroui as a "moral crisis" which "culminated in a period of anguished self-criticism, a searching reappraisal of postwar Arab culture and political practice".[16] Reactions to this "setback" (*naksa*), as it is termed by Arab writers, varied widely: from a lapse into silence for several years to an expression of the most violent anger. And, as we draw ever closer to the present, one's view of how much this situation has changed or developed will depend on a number of perspectives. The 1973 crossing of the Suez Canal by Egyptian forces, for example, has been regarded in official Egyptian quarters as a turning point in modern Arab history. It may well have been a psychological boost for the Egyptian people and therefore of considerable significance, but its impact on the rest of the Arab world has been minimal. On the other hand, the continuing tragedy of the Palestinian people, the Camp David Accords, the bitter civil strife in Lebanon, and a host of other factors, seem regrettably to contribute to "an increasingly pronounced polarization of forces", as Laroui notes in his book with the significant title of *The crisis of the Arab intellectual*.[17]

The preceding pages have attempted to present in a very generalised and abbreviated form some of the most salient social and political features which characterise the history of the various societies of the Arab world since the Second World War. In keeping with the topic of this book, we have exemplified some of the trends with allusions to and quotations from certain novels. It is now time to invert the process, examining the novels themselves and observing what techniques they use in order to treat the themes already mentioned and others from within the society itself.

2. *The novels: themes and techniques*

The course of a single year (around 1939[18]) saw the publication in Lebanon of *al-Raghīf* ("The loaf") by Tawfīq Yūsuf

[16] *The crisis of the Arab intellectual*, Berkeley: University of California Press, 1976, p. viii. See also Muḥammad Barādī, in *al-Ādāb* (Feb.-March 1980), 3.

[17] Laroui, *ibid.*

[18] Those scholars who labour with the practices (or nonpractices) of Arab-world publishers regarding publication data will realise how difficult it

ʿAwwād, in Iraq of *al-Duktūr Ibrāhīm* ("Doctor Ibrāhīm") by Dhū al-Nūn Ayyūb, and in Egypt of *ʿAbath al-aqdār* ("Mockery of the fates") by Najīb Maḥfūẓ. All three of these writers had been producing works of short fiction during the 1930s, but most critics are agreed that the authors of the novels listed above begin to show a particular awareness of experiments made previously within each national tradition and in the Arabic novel tradition as a whole and to demonstrate an ability to employ a new level of technical expertise in the composition of their works.

ʿAwwād (born in 1911), a journalist and diplomat, uses his very popular novel to give a graphic picture of Arab resistance to the Turks during the First World War. The hero, Sāmī ʿĀṣim, a fervent Arab nationalist, takes refuge in a cave when he is hunted by the Turks. His beloved, Zayna, brings him food and information. However, the location of his hideaway is revealed, and he is captured and tortured by the Turks. At the outbreak of the Arab Revolt of 1916, Sāmī is believed to be dead. In revenge, Zayna allows herself to be enticed to the Turkish commander's house where she shoots him. She then joins a group of Arab saboteurs and learns that Sāmī is not dead but leading the Arab forces in their fight against the Turks. He dies in the fighting and thus is unable to be with Zayna as the victorious Arabs re-enter their villages, having ousted the Turks and won back for themselves the loaf of bread to eat which provides the work with its title.

Within the context of Arab aspirations in the 1930s and 1940s, the popularity of this work is understandable; it does indeed reflect the concerns of the society within which it was written. In many ways, it emerges in much the same way as the historical-romantic novels set in earlier periods of Middle Eastern history which we described above. However, as Suhayl Idrīs, the editor of *al-Ādāb* notes, there is a significant development in technique:

> The author displays a particular awareness of novelistic technique. There is a coherent structure to the work which leads the reader through the various events with a good deal of confidence.

is to pinpoint precise chronological information. The situation has improved in recent years, but even so, I have often been compelled in writing this work to rely on secondary sources for dates of publication of novels and works of criticism.

Furthermore, the framework within which the story is treated shows a good deal of focus and artistic acumen which allows the events of the narrative to be portrayed in a gradual progression of considerable subtlety.[19]

The second of these novels, that of Dhū al-Nūn Ayyūb, also treats one of the major themes of the *nahḍa* to which we alluded above: the impact of Western culture on those Arabs who go to Europe to study and the return to their homeland. The work paints a sordid picture of opportunism, as a young Iraqi with a Persian father is sent to England for his university education, totally assimilates British values, marries an English girl and acquires a doctorate. He then returns home, and by peddling influence and prejudice manages to secure himself a position in the Ministry of Agriculture. He joins all the right societies and organisations in order to gain the attention of his Minister and of the British, and then proceeds to acquire as much prestige and money as he can, mostly at the expense of his colleagues. When their enmity towards him and his own awareness of his political vulnerability reaches a certain point, he transfers his funds out of the country and takes out American citizenship. Once again, the socio-critical purpose of this work is not handled with the subtlety of some later works, but we are led to believe that Ayyūb himself was made to suffer internal exile in Iraq as a result of departmental intrigue.[20] This fact, together with the historical circumstances in which the novel was conceived, no doubt contributed to the somewhat excessive fervour with which the author portrays the evil qualities of his hero.

Both ʿAwwād and Ayyūb have written other novels, although they seem to concentrate rather more on the short story genre. Ayyūb's *al-Yad wa-al-arḍ wa-al-māʾ* ("Hand, earth and water", 1947) is, as the title suggests, another rather didactic work, this time involving the struggle undertaken by some professional people from the city to break the stranglehold of provincial landowners over the lives of the peasants. ʿAwwād's most recent novel, *Ṭawāḥīn Bayrūt* ("Treadmills of Beirut",

[19] *al-Ādāb* (Feb. 1957), 15. See also Jūrj (George) Sālim, *al-Mughāmara al-riwāʾiyya*, Damascus: Manshūrāt Ittiḥād al-Kuttāb al-ʿArab, 1973, 103-7.

[20] Yūsuf ʿIzz al-Dīn, *al-Riwāya fī al-ʿIrāq*, 210-11. See also Jamīl Saʿīd, *Naẓarāt fī al-tayyārāt al-adabiyya*, 33-8.

1972[21]) once again undertakes to portray the problems within the society of his native Lebanon; on this occasion, the period is that which followed the 1967 war with Israel. Against the background of the threat of Israeli invasions of Southern Lebanon, a young girl of Shiʿite background comes to Beirut and becomes involved in a complex web of intersectarian relationships. The translator of this work into English describes in an introduction the way in which he was forced to dodge the gunfire during the civil war in Lebanon in order to reach the author's house and discuss the translation with him. Those brief comments can serve as perhaps the most effective possible commentary on the content and import of this carefully crafted and highly effective work.

Of this trio of novelists—this "generation of '39" perhaps—it is Najīb Maḥfūẓ who has written the most in novel form and who has earned the widest repute. Indeed, he is without doubt the Arab world's most illustrious novelist. When his famous *al-Thulāthiyya* ("The trilogy", 1956-7) appeared, it was immediately realised that here was an Arab novelist of the first rank. His earlier works, of which *The trilogy* may be considered the culmination at that time, were avidly read, and the appearance of each new novel by him was the occasion for a whole series of articles and reviews in all the literary periodicals of the region. He has been the subject of a number of books and theses in Arabic and European languages.[22] It is a non-Egyptian, ʿAbd al-Raḥmān al-Yāghī in his work *al-Juhūd al-riwā'iyya*, who entitles a chapter "The phase when narrative art becomes established, in other words, the Najīb Maḥfūẓ phase".[23] This, coupled with the size and temporal spread of his oeuvre—his latest novel entitled *al-Ḥubb wa-al-qināʿ* ("Love and the veil", 1980) has just appeared—forces us to consider his artistry and its impact at some length.

First novels are not, of course, necessarily representative of

[21] Translated by Leslie McLoughlin as *Death in Beirut*, London: Heinemann, 1976.

[22] Most notable in Arabic are: Ghālī Shukrī, *al-Muntamī*, Cairo: Dār al-Maʿārif, 1969; Nabīl Rāghib, *Qaḍiyyat al-shakl al-fannī ʿinda Najīb Maḥfūẓ*, Cairo: al-Hay'a al-Miṣriyya al-ʿāmma li-al-kitāb, 1975; Maḥmūd al-Rabīʿī, *Qirā'at al-riwāya*, Cairo; Dār al-Maʿārif, 1974; and ʿAbd al-Muḥsin Ṭāhā Badr, *Najīb Maḥfūẓ: al-Ru'yā wa-al-adāt*, Cairo: Dār al-Thaqāfa li-al-Ṭibāʿa wa-al-Nashr, 1978. In English, Somekh, *The changing rhythm*.

[23] Beirut: Dār al-ʿAwda, 1972.

their author's best work, and such is certainly the case with Maḥfūẓ's *'Abath al-aqdār*. It is the first of three novels which depict incidents from periods of ancient Egyptian history, a subject on which Maḥfūẓ had translated a work from English into Arabic in the early 1930s.[24] While this translation activity no doubt prompted his interest in the subject (and, indeed, he appears to have formulated plans for a whole series of similar works on ancient Egypt), the result falls very much within the framework of other historical novels written earlier, with a great deal of action and little penetration beneath the surface of the characters. However, *'Abath al-aqdār* does not represent Maḥfūẓ's first effort at fictional writing. He had written a large number of stories during the 1930s (many of which are now to be found in the collection *Hams al-junūn* ("The whisper of madness"), the dating of which is problematic[25]). These stories show some of Maḥfūẓ's concerns with contemporary issues—the title story, for example, deals with the question of the nature of madness.[26] During the early 1940s, years of war and political unrest in Egypt, Maḥfūẓ turned his attention away from the ancient history of his country and applied himself to the issues of the contemporary period on a broader canvas, that of the realistic novel. In a series of novels, the first of which was published in 1945 and the last, *The trilogy*, after a pause in 1956-7, Maḥfūẓ depicts with loving attention to detail the lives of Egyptians in various quarters of the city of Cairo. The impact of these works reminds us of Lionel Trilling's remark that the novel can serve as

> an especially useful agent of the moral imagination. ... the literary form which most directly reveals to us the complexity, the difficulty, and the interest of life in society, and best instructs us in our human variety and contradiction.[27]

The chaos and corruption in local politics are well illustrated in *al-Qāhira al-jadīda* ("Modern Cairo", 1945 ?[28]) which depicts the varied lives of three students in the early 1930s. On the international level, we see the effects of foreign occupation and

[24] See Somekh, 42, 60 ff. for a discussion of these novels.

[25] *Ibid.*, 46 n. 2.

[26] Cf. Kamal Abu Deeb's discussion of the poetry of Adūnīs, "The perplexity of the all-knowing", *Mundus Artium* X/1 (1977), 163-81.

[27] *The liberal imagination*, New York: Scribner, 1940 and 1950, p. vii.

[28] For the problem of dating these works, see Somekh, 198-9.

dominance in both *Khān al-Khalīlī* and *Zuqāq al-Midaqq* (1945 and 1947 respectively, both of them significantly place names). In the latter work, ʿAbbās the reticent barber plies his trade at the British barracks so that he can earn enough money to marry his beloved Ḥamīda who also lives in the *zuqāq* (alley), a microcosm representing the problems of Egyptian society as a whole. However, he returns to discover that Ḥamīda has had more ambitious goals and has gone out in search of gain herself. In the process she has come to the attention of a pimp who trains her to act as a whore for British soldiers. When ʿAbbās finds her at a bar surrounded by soldiers towards the end of the work and disfigures her face with a broken bottle, he is pummelled to death as his friend stands hopelessly by. The moral is clear enough.

While crime is rarely made to pay in these novels, virtue brings few rewards either; the implication is that the problems facing the bourgeoisie who are the primary focus of the author's attention are too severe for such a "happy ending". A case in point is *Bidāya wa-nihāya* ("Beginning and end", 1950). The novel begins with the death of a minor civil servant who leaves behind a family consisting of his wife, three sons and a daughter. The story concerns the attempt of the mother and her children to better their lot in life in spite of the totally-inadequate pension on which they are supposed to survive. The eldest son is already leading the life of a profligate, dope peddler and pimp. The bulk of the narrative concerns the two younger sons, one of whom aspires to be a teacher while the other goes to military college. The daughter, Nafīsa, falls in love with a local boy, but he marries someone else. She is gradually drawn into prostitution in order to help in the support of the family, although they have no idea that she is not getting the money from her work as a seamstress. Eventually however, she is arrested for prostitution, and her horrified brother, Ḥasanayn, has to go to the police station to collect her. Nafīsa's attempts to explain herself are in vain, and her brother agrees to her proposal that she kill herself. This she does by jumping off a bridge into the Nile. When her body has been recovered, he too jumps into the river.

This pessimistic "agent of the moral imagination" is a work of considerable length, but from that point of view it merely serves as a precedent for *The trilogy*, each volume of which is named after a different quarter of the city, *Bayn al-qaṣrayn*, *Qaṣr al-shawq*, and *al-Sukkariyya*. This huge work of over 1,500 pages traces the life, beliefs, tragedies and loves of the family of ʿAbd al-Jawwād in the period between the two World Wars and into the Second World War. Like the great novelistic sagas of Tolstoy, Galsworthy, Trollope, Hugo and others, it operates on numerous levels. The setting of each volume in a different part of the city illustrates well the transformations within society, of which the fate of this family is a example. From the first volume, in which the father exerts a tyrannical hold over his family while employing a double standard with regard to his own behaviour, we proceed to the second, in which the second son confronts his father's traditional beliefs with the evolutionary theories which he is studying in Teachers' College. In the third volume, boys and girls are studying together at university. Two of the grandsons of the first generation finish up in jail, one as a Communist, the other as a member of the Muslim Brethren. There could hardly be a better example of the feuds and divisions in Egyptian society and the sense of alienation among intellectuals which marked the period before the 1952 Revolution.[29] And yet, the main protagonist of this work is surely Time itself. The manner in which Maḥfūẓ holds together this vast historical survey of Egyptian society in the process of change recalls Georg Lukacs' remarks on Flaubert's *L'éducation sentimentale*:

> The unrestricted, uninterrupted flow of time is the unifying principle of the homogeneity that rubs the sharp edges off each heterogeneous fragment and establishes a relationship—albeit an irrational and inexpressible one—between them. Time brings order into the chaos of men's lives and gives it the semblance of a spontaneously flowering, organic entity; characters having no apparent meaning appear, establish relations with one another, break them off, disappear again without any meaning having been revealed.[30]

The trilogy was completed in April 1952 after five years of research and writing, but was not published until 1956. Quite apart from the problems of publishing such a voluminous work, there was also the fact of the new Revolution, the course and impact of which was far from clear at the outset. Maḥfūẓ ceased writing fiction for a while and turned his attention to another

[29] As Laroui notes, *The crisis of the Arab intellectual*, 120.
[30] *The theory of the novel*, 125.

love of his, the cinema.[31] His next fictional work, *Awlād ḥāratinā* ("Children of our quarter", 1959—serialised in *al-Ahrām*) is an allegorical survey of mankind's religious history and represents something of an anomaly in his novelistic output, although it did serve notice of a change in both theme and technique. The 1960s saw the appearance of another series of novels which are linked by similar treatments of theme. Here the emphasis shifts from the complex fabric of society itself to the equally complex world of the individual and the sense of alienation felt by modern man when faced with the pressures of life in today's world. This phase in Maḥfūẓ's career is marked most obviously by a more economical treatment of the description of place, but also evident are an increased awareness of the psychological dimensions of character through the use of internal monologue and stream-of-consciousness and a subtle and effective use of symbols. The characters who people these works find themselves for one reason or another out of place in Egyptian society. This is probably most obvious in the case of ʿĪsā al-Dabbāgh, a senior government official under the old royal régime, whose life collapses around him in the wake of the Revolution, the purges of corrupt civil servants, and his own unwillingness to face up to the realities of the situation. *Al-Summān wa-al-kharīf* ("Quail and autumn", 1962) symbolises not only his personal withdrawal to Alexandria after his fall but also the fact that life is carrying on without him. Saʿīd Mahrān is the thief in *al-Liṣṣ wa-al-kilāb* ("The thief and the dogs", 1961) who feels betrayed not only by his wife who has deserted him while he was in prison but also by Ra'ūf ʿIlwān, a journalist who has abandoned his former radical positions towards society and the rights of the poor in favour of a life of prosperity. Mahrān's attempts to kill those who have betrayed him fail, and he is hounded down by the police with their dogs. The novel ends, tellingly, in a cemetery.

This series of works contains many adumbrations of the unease which, as we suggested above, marked the decade of the 1960s. This criticism reaches its peak in *Mīrāmār* (the name of a pension, 1967[32]), in which the character most associated with

[31] For which he wrote a number of scenarios and scripts. See Hāshim al-Naḥḥās, *Najīb Maḥfūẓ ʿalā al-shāsha*, Cairo: al-Hay'a al-Miṣriyya al-ʿĀmma li-al-Kitāb, 1975, 28.

[32] Translated by Fatma Moussa-Mahmoud, London: Heinemann, and Washington: Three Continents Press, 1978.

the Revolution is involved in a scheme to swindle his company out of some of its property. This fact and the comments of other guests at the Pension Mīrāmār do not paint a rosy picture of the course of the Egyptian Revolution.

Maḥfūẓ's first venture into the novel form after the June War of 1967 can hardly be termed a novel at all: *al-Marāyā* ("Mirrors", 1972). In this work, many of the criticisms which had been suggested in earlier novels were now, in the spirit of the post-1967 period, made more explicit.[33] However, the increased candour of this and subsequent works has not, in my opinion, been matched by that same artistry and technique which so characterised his earlier works.[34] Maḥfūẓ on many occasions expressed his discomfort with the directions in which Sādāt's Egypt seemed to be going,[35] and one can only say that the arrant commercialisation of much of the cultural sector in Egypt in recent times does not appear to have stimulated him to produce novels to rival those of his earlier years. The proliferation of characters and the copious use of dialogue in his most recent works of fiction give them very much the appearance of what they rapidly become, namely scenarios for films. While some critics may wish to see this as a new "phase" in Maḥfūẓ's novelistic career, it seems to me to represent a rather saddening wane in both application and technique. The fact that his most recent novel, *al-Ḥubb wa-al-qināʿ*, has been selling very poorly suggests that the reading public in Egypt and the rest of the Arab world may now be turning to a younger generation of writers of fiction.

If our assessment of Maḥfūẓ's recent works is a harsh one, that in no way diminishes our view of him as the major pioneer in the development of a mature tradition in the realistic novel. On the technical level he has demonstrated the careful planning of a meticulous craftsman in the construction of plot, while with regard to characterisation he has been able to use his training in philosophy and his wide readings in Western literature to good advantage. The views of Robert Scholes and Robert Kellogg in *The nature of narrative* seem appropriate in assessing his skills:

[33] Translated by Roger Allen, Chicago: Bibliotheca Islamica, 1977.

[34] See *idem*, "Some recent works of Najīb Maḥfūẓ", *JARCE* XIV (1977), 101-10.

[35] See *idem*, "Egyptian fiction and drama in the 1970s", *Edebiyat*, I/2 (1976), 221-3.

> Of the giants of the age of the novel can we not say that the principal thing which unites them is the special care for characterization which is inextricably bound up with the creation of character from the facets of the artist's own psyche?[36]

With these skills at his command, he has addressed himself to the problems of the society in which he lives and to the larger issues facing modern man with a sweep which reflects his own broad reading in the literatures of the world. On the matter of style, he has steadfastly resisted the trend towards the use of colloquial in dialogue, although this has not prevented him from using individual words culled from that source in order to lend some local colour to his characters. While certain changes are evident in stylistic technique between the realistic and more symbolic phases, the lexicon remains relatively restricted in comparison with many other modern Arab novelists. The style is very much that of the methodical craftsman, the civil servant rather than the more impulsive and even poetic creator. And, while making this observation, we should also add that Maḥfūẓ restricts his milieux to those with which he is familiar: the scene is, more often than not, the lives of the bourgeois, bureaucrat class. With this in mind, style and content are well wedded.

The name of Najīb Maḥfūẓ has dominated the sphere of the Arabic novel during a large part of the period under discussion in this chapter. As I write these words, he has written twenty-three novels and nine collections of short stories, a large output by any gauge one cares to use. Many of these books have gone into several editions (three of the novels are in their ninth) and they are widely read throughout the Middle East. If some of this outpouring of narrative is less effective and popular than the rest, and if recent works seem to show a decline, that can still not diminish Maḥfūẓ's status as the figure-head of this phase in the development of the Arabic novel.

In tracing the novelistic career of Maḥfūẓ in some detail, we have followed one strand of the tradition right through to the present day, that strand which focuses its lens on the society of its time, whether through the highly-detailed medium of social realism or via the reflected and often more subtle vision of the individual within society. From previous chapters, however, it will be recalled that realism was by no means the first mode to

[36] London: Oxford University Press, 1966, 192.

be applied within the Arabic novel tradition; it was preceded by both the historical and romantic traditions.

Within the general process of the *nahḍa*, involving a rediscovery of the classical heritage and a reassertion of national identity, the historical novel played an important role with its combined pedagogical and entertainment functions. In Egypt, for example, the period following the 1919 Revolution saw an upsurge in national pride, and the sensational discoveries in 1922 in the tomb of Tutankhamun made this sense of history even more intense. Maḥfūẓ's own translation of an Egyptological work into Arabic and his initial historical novels may perhaps be seen as part of this increasing awareness of historical roots which finds its clearest expression in the so-called "Pharaonism" movement (seen at its most obvious, perhaps, in Tawfīq al-Ḥakīm's novel, *'Awdat al-rūḥ*). As Yūsuf 'Izz al-Dīn notes, the same process is evident in Iraq.[37] During the inter-war period and in the 1940s, many writers produced historical novels set in both ancient and mediaeval times, but since that time this particular type of novel has suffered a significant decline. Modern Arab writers continue to make use of history in their fictional works (as we will note with reference to Maḥfūẓ's *Tharthara fawq al-Nīl* in the next chapter). However, the purpose is no longer merely to entertain with a plethora of action but to use the past to illustrate and draw morals for the present and future. When Jamāl al-Ghīṭānī, a young Egyptian novelist, uses texts from a historian of the Mamlūk period in his novel *al-Zīnī Barakāt* (a man's name, 1976), his purpose is to pass sardonic and highly critical comment on civil liberties in Egypt in the 1960s and 1970s rather than to put the events of several centuries earlier into a more palatable form.

The historical trend has been followed in the early stages by the romantic, with Haykal's *Zaynab* as an initial example. This trend had been and has remained extremely popular, and, as 'Abd al-Muḥsin Ṭāhā Badr ruefully notes, the prevalence of the realistic genre as the favoured type in the tradition of the artistic novel has done nothing to diminish the popularity of the romantic trend:

[37] *al-Riwāya fī al-'Irāq*, 160. For examples from Egypt, see Sakkut, *The Egyptian novel and its main trends*, 46-84.

They continue to exist because readers exist who do not enjoy having their consciousnesses raised but merely want to be entertained. In all societies, there exist semi-literate types who are ready to pander to the taste of this readership. Many such readers have recently been drawn away from the entertainment novel in the direction of radio plays and films, and most recently of all, to television.[38]

Iḥsān 'Abd al-Quddūs, the famous son of a famous mother, the actress Rose al-Yūsuf, earned a wide reputation for himself by writing a whole series of works of romantic fiction which broached the subject of the structure of the family and the position of women in a provocative way, making him perhaps in fiction the analogue of Nizār Qabbānī in modern Arabic poetry. While there are many other novelists of this kind (of whom Yūsuf al-Sibāʿī and 'Abd al-Ḥalīm 'Abdallāh are the most worthy of mention), none has been able to match the popularity of 'Abd al-Quddūs.

These novels and novelists may reflect certain periods in the history and development of modern Arabic culture, but, as we have tried to show at the beginning of this chapter, recent decades have witnessed tremendous changes in the fabric of Arab societies. It is natural therefore that the novel has been called upon to fulfill that role which it performs better than any other literary genre, that of serving as a mirror and critic of the society within which it is conceived. This no doubt also accounts for the relegation of the historical and romantic trends to ancillary positions within the tradition of the Arabic novel in this period.

The call which Commitment made for the involvement of literature in the development of Arab society is naturally reflected in writings about the novel. Ḥalīm Barakāt, for example, expresses his views in this way:

Contemporary Arab writers have been pre-occupied with themes of struggle, revolution, liberation, emancipation, rebellion, alienation. A writer could not be a part of Arab society and yet not concern himself with change. To be oblivious to tyranny, injustice, poverty, deprivation, victimization, repression, is insensitively proper. I would even say that writing about Arab society without concerning oneself with change is a sort of *engagement* in irrelevances.[39]

[38] *Taṭawwur al-riwāya*, 169.

[39] "Arabic novels and social transformation", in *Studies in modern Arabic literature* ed. R.C. Ostle, Warminster, England: Aris and Phillips, 1975, 126-7.

Elsewhere, Barakāt categorises recent fiction according to the way in which the author broaches the theme of societal change, while admitting that his own aims for society as a novelist are revolutionary.[40] Within such terms of reference, most of the novels of Maḥfūẓ, for example, emerge as "novels of exposure", a category which "exposes the weaknesses and limitations of the society and its institutions without exhibiting any real commitment to the cause of restructuring the existing order".[41] It is a somewhat controversial opinion to suggest that Maḥfūẓ is not really concerned with societal change in his novels of the 1940s and early 1950s (discussed above), but one can at least agree with Barakāt that the novels which he includes in his category of "novels of revolutionary change" are far more explicit in outlining their social agenda. Many of those novels will be discussed in what follows (although not under Barakāt's rubrics), but in concluding this brief discussion of his approach one may perhaps suggest that the terms of reference which he uses tend to downplay the importance of artistic subtleties in assessing the achievement of the novel genre.

Other critics have employed the thematic approach in their assessment of the Arabic novel in recent times. One such is Shukrī 'Ayyād, who uses the following categories: those which seek for some kind of national identity; those which concern themselves with the passage of time; those which deal with the individual and his experience within society; those which adopt a critical stance; and lastly, those which investigate aspects of the metaphysical.[42] Still other critics have preferred some kind of blend of the thematic approach and the broader categories which we used earlier (such as historical, romantic and realistic) as they endeavour to sift and assess current trends.[43] In spite of the different approaches used in these various surveys, a number of themes emerge which have obviously been primary concerns of Arab novelists during the past two or three decades; the rest

[40] *Visions of social reality in the contemporary Arabic novel*, Georgetown: Center for Contemporary Arabic Studies, Seminar Paper No. 1, 1977, 36.

[41] *Ibid.*, 28.

[42] "al-Riwāya al-'Arabiyya al-mu'āṣira wa-azmat al-ḍamīr al-'Arabī", *'Ālam al-Fikr* III/3 (Oct.-Dec. 1972), 619-48.

[43] E.g. Khālida Sa'īd, "al-Riwāya al-'Arabiyya bayn 1920-1972", *Mawāqif* 28 (Summer 1974), 75-88, and Vial, *EI*² art. "Ḳiṣṣa".

of this chapter will devote itself to a discussion of those novels which deal with these particular subjects.

If we bear in mind the fact that the tragedy of the Palestinians and the confrontation with Israel has been a bitter reality for the Arabs throughout this period, it will come as no surprise to learn that it is also one of the principal themes of novels. Some have dealt in a direct fashion with the fighting between Arabs and Israelis, and the attention paid to the events of 1948 and 1967 not only suggests the extreme importance which they have in modern Arab history but also underlines the somewhat diminished significance which novelists seem to attach to the Suez Crisis of 1956 and the October Crossing and its aftermath in 1973. With regard to the latter, it is true, as Vial notes, that the Moroccan novelist Mubārak Rabīʿ sets his novel *Rifqat al-silāḥ wa-al-qamar* ("Company of arms and the moon", 1976) amid the fighting on the Golan Heights in Syria, but the major purpose seems to be to register the presence of Moroccan troops in the conflict and in any case the work does not match the quality of his other (prize-winning) contributions to the genre.

Ḥalīm Barakāt, the sociologist and critic whose views we have cited above, visited Amman following the Six-Day War of June 1967, and, as a result of that visit and interviews which he conducted at that time, he was able to give us a *cinéma vérité* view of the fighting and terrible plight of Arab refugees during those six days in his novel, *ʿAwdat al-ṭāʾir ilā al-baḥr*, examined in detail below. An earlier work, the prophetically-named *Sittat ayyām* ("Six days", 1961), was set within the context of the 1948 fighting. The same chronological time frame of six days is used to portray the fate of the seaside town of Dayr al-Baḥr as it is besieged by attacking Israeli forces. Nor does the similarity end there: this work also contains a reference to the legend of the Flying Dutchman, although in this earlier work it serves as just one of a number of citations from European literature, whereas in the later work it forms the motto theme against which the events take place.[44] In *Sittat ayyām* the attempts of the villagers to organise resistance to the Israeli siege are seen through the eyes of Suhayl, the novel's hero, but the action of the novel is not confined to a recounting of the build-up towards the final attack on the town. Through a generous use of interior monologue, the reader is admitted to the thoughts of several of

[44] Beirut; Dār Majallat Shiʿr, 1961, 17.

the major characters, in particular Suhayl, the two girls with whom he consorts—the worldly-wise Lamyā, and the initially cloistered but later liberated Nāhida—and Farīd, the leader of the local resistance forces. Within this framework, the author seems unable to avoid the temptation to comment on faults in the society, and this leads to sometimes lengthy digressions on the general backwardness of the country, the problems of intermarriage, and the general feeling of alienation among the younger generation.[45] Thus, while the descriptions of the attempts at resistance and of the love scenes are handled with an effective vividness, many of the characters emerge more as stereotypes of particular forces in society than as real people, and they are not well integrated into the structure of the plot. Indeed, the narrative seems to be divided rather artificially into episodes of village description, others of intimate and explicit love scenes and still others devoted to action, infiltration and fighting. The result seems unnatural and lacks cohesion. This said, however, it should be added that Barakāt here shows a felicitous use of symbol and style which were to emerge in equally, if not more, forceful fashion in his later novel. The symbol of the village clock which has been immobile for years serves as a constant and intrusive reminder of the inability or unwillingness of the society to change.[46] The author's use of heightened language—truncated sentences and phrases and staccato images in the historical present—during the funeral procession of the resistance fighters and the vivid scenes of love-making is especially striking.[47]

Barakāt's novels depict the two major confrontations between Israel and the Arab states during the period under discussion in this chapter. While the characters in these novels and others operate against Israel from the Arab world, still other works depict the fight—in actions and words—as it goes on within Israel itself. Tawfīq Fayyāḍ's *Majmūʿa 778* ("778 Group", 1975) describes the activities of a Fedayeen group made up of ex-fishermen from ʿAkkā who are given authorisation from the High Command in Amman to undertake guerilla activity inside Israel.[48] Emile Ḥabībī, on the other hand, has

[45] *Sittat ayyām*, 25, 36-7, 90-6.
[46] *Ibid.*, 10, 25, 71, 114, 132.
[47] *Ibid.*, 113, 100, 143 ff.
[48] See ʿAbd al-Karīm al-Ashtar, *Dirāsa fī adab al-nakba*, n.p.: Dār al-Fikr, 1975, 105-38.

been engaged in a different kind of battle, attempting in two works to show the bitter ironies of daily life in Israel for the Arab citizens of that country. While *Sudāsiyyat al-ayyām al-sitta* ("Sextet on the six days", 1969) is a bitter-sweet description of six separate encounters between Arabs in Israel and their relatives in neighbouring states, his later work, *al-Waqā'iʿ al-gharība fī ikhtifā' Saʿīd Abī al-Naḥs al-mutashā'il* ("The peculiar events surrounding the disappearance of the ill-starred Saʿīd the Pessoptimist", 1974, 1977), is not only a wonderfully sardonic account of life in Israel, but, as the wordiness of the title suggests, an evocation of the picaresque *maqāma* genre initiated in the tenth century by al-Hamadhānī and revived in modern times by al-Muwayliḥī (see above, chapter 2).[49] In fact, Saʿīd's claim in the first chapter to have encountered extra-terrestrial beings sets up precisely the same narrative-distancing based on either time or space which had been used as a device by both al-Muwayliḥī and Ḥāfiẓ Ibrāhīm in their criticisms of society earlier in the century.[50] The work is subdivided into three books, the first and last given the girl's name Yuʿād, a word implying "return", while the central book is entitled Bāqiya, also a girl's name with the sense of "remaining"; the significance of this choice of titles need not be emphasised. However, the work succeeds in its purpose of giving us a kaleidoscopic view of the life of an Arab in Israel through the use of extremely short chapters which afford ample opportunity for changes of pace and scene and encourage terse and sardonic comment. The result of this montage is a truly picaresque and sometimes farcical work of fiction which manages to show great originality while conveying its often bitter message with a tragicomic force.

Other Palestinian novelists have taken as their theme the plight of their fellow-countrymen in exile throughout the Arab world and elsewhere, and the various ways in which their longing for their homeland and the inevitable sense of alienation which they feel find expression. Of these writers we would single out Ghassān Kanafānī and Jabrā Ibrāhīm Jabrā.

[49] See le Gassick, "The luckless Palestinian", *MEJ* XXXIV/2 (Spring 1980), 215-23.

[50] Emile Ḥabībī, *al-Waqā'iʿ al-gharība fī ikhtifā' Saʿīd Abī al-Naḥs al-mutashā'il*, Jerusalem: Manshūrāt Ṣalāḥ al-Dīn, 1977, 13; see also Allen, "*Ḥadīth ʿĪsā ibn Hishām* by Muḥammad al-Muwailiḥī: a reconsideration", *JAL* I (1970), 99.

Kanafānī is the novelist whose name is most closely associated with the Palestinian cause, not only in that Palestinians occupy the central position in his fictional works but also in that he served as a spokesman for the Popular Front for the Liberation of Palestine. It was presumably because of this rôle (and perhaps the forceful effect of his novels) that he was assassinated in Beirut in 1972 when his car was booby-trapped. Jabrā, now resident in Baghdad, places his fellow-countrymen on a broader canvas (he is, in fact, also a painter and art critic), not only within the context of Arab society but as part of a comprehensive study of inter-cultural connections and the alienation of modern man. All this is achieved with a breadth of vision and sophistication which reflect the author's considerable erudition.

Kanafānī's most famous work is undoubtedly *Rijāl fī al-shams* ("Men in the sun", 1963). In this short and powerful work in which the symbolic functions seem often akin to allegory, three Palestinians attempt the difficult journey across the desert to Kuwait where they hope to find employment. The desert here is a totally inhospitable environment, and the Palestinians in their quest are pounded mercilessly by the desert sun. To serve these travelers and others like them, a whole group of middle-men are available near the border to convey them into Kuwait illegally and to steer them clear of marauding Bedouin who will otherwise rob them of everything they own. The three individuals are picked up by Abū Khayzurān, the driver of a water-tanker who agrees to take them over the border inside the water-tank. It emerges that Abū Khayzurān has been rendered impotent by a previous war wound, and, with this fact in mind, the events which ensue give an additional element of absurdity to the dire plight of the men in the tank. At the Iraqi border all goes well. But when the tanker reaches the Kuwaiti post, the driver is delayed while the customs official teases him about his girl friend in Baghdad. Fatal minutes pass, and when Abū Khayzurān eventually opens the tank, his three passengers are dead. In a desperate move of clear and devastating symbolic significance, he takes the corpses to the communal garbage dump and abandons them there after removing all their valuables. Why, he wonders, did they not beat on the side of the tank?[51]

[51] Kanafānī, *al-Āthār al-kāmila*, Beirut: Dār al-Ṭalīʿa, 1972. 152.

The powerful way in which this work depicts the plight of the Palestinian in his exile within the Arab world has given it a wide readership. But, while the message is important, and no more so than in the case of Kanafānī, the work is carefully constructed so as to give maximum impact to the concluding events. Each character is introduced as a separate individual representing a different aspect of Palestinian life, and it is only when they join Abū Khayzurān in their fateful journey together that the experience becomes unified. Thereafter, events move swiftly, and the symbolic supersedes the individual. Indeed, one may criticise the novel as a whole for giving the reader a rather two-dimensional view of the characters. That having been said, however, it must be added that the imagery used to convey the impact of the symbols, particularly the descriptions of the desert and the unbearable heat of the sun, is couched in a language which is clear and effective.

Another novel, *'Āid ilā Ḥayfā* ("Going back to Haifa", 1969), portrays a different aspect of Emile Ḥabībī's theme of the Arabs living in Israel. An Arab couple return to their home to discover that their long-lost son, left behind when they fled from their homes, has been brought up by a European Jewish couple as an Israeli. Here again the situation allows for a discussion of the more obvious aspects of the Palestinian tragedy. In other novels (and particularly *Mā tabaqqā lakum*, discussed in detail in the following chapter) there are signs of a growing sophistication in technique which lead one to suspect that, had he lived, Kanafānī would have made further significant contributions to the development of the tradition of the Arabic novel. Even so, what he has left us is a whole series of valuable insights in fiction into the sad, complex and often recalcitrant world of the Palestinians in their various havens of exile.

Baghdad, Rome, Jerusalem, Beirut, Oxford, all these are the scenes of events in the novels of Jabrā whose treatment of the fate of his fellow-Palestinians seems to reflect the words of his close friend, the late poet Tawfīq Ṣāyigh:

Approaching, but no entry
travelling, but no arrival:
without it there is no entry
and you do not carry it
therefore no entry.[52]

The characters who people Jabrā's novels are in the main intellectuals: writers, artists, members of the social élite, radical politicians, and the like. They live a life of alienation, and Palestinian and non-Palestinian alike, they aspire towards a newer and better existence so as to escape from the problems of life in contemporary Arab society. This applies as much to the female characters as it does to the male; in several of the novels, the women revolt against the traditional values of society as a way of expiating their own personal frustrations. It is the *'ashā'iriyya* or tribalistic attitudes of Iraqi society which stand in the way of the happiness of 'Iṣām and Lumā in *al-Safīna* ("The ship", 1969), Jabrā's novel which we examine in detail in the next chapter, and much the same situation is portrayed in *Hunters in a narrow street* (1960) which Jabrā wrote in English and in which the young girl, Sulāfa, is kept cloistered by her pietistic father. Also given a vivid portrayal in his novels is the barbaric way in which many of these intellectuals are treated by the governing authorities. We have already cited the outpouring of wrath unleashed by Walīd Mas'ūd in Jabrā's latest novel *al-Baḥth 'an Walīd Mas'ūd*, which provides the best example of the author's views on this subject, but the experiences of Maḥmūd Rāshid in *al-Safīna* are, at least by implication, equally gruesome. And in the case of each one of the novels, the future and the hopes of a better life so avidly sought by the characters are always left hanging in the air. In *Walīd Mas'ūd* and *al-Safīna* a great deal remains ambiguous and unresolved after the final page. And, although it was written in English, we will again cite from his *Hunters in a narrow street* as an excellent example of this phenomenon. The final paragraph reads:

In the long months that followed, while we waited, while the Adnans and the Husains and the Towfiqs impaled themselves on rows of political and social swords, the crows and the kites in squawking formations flew over the palm groves of a slowly refurbished land.

Jabrā is not only a novelist, but a poet and critic as well. A

[52] "Poem 24", from *al-Qaṣīda K* (Beirut, 1960), trans. Issa J. Boullata in *Modern Arab poets 1950–1975*, Washington: Three Continents Press, 1976, 146.

major feature of his novels is thus (not unnaturally) his use of language, imagery and symbols. The short extract given above, with its effective use of metaphor, is but a small example of a stylistic trait which is a hallmark of his fictional works. Apart from examples of his own poetry and colourful descriptions of background (such as the sea in *al-Safīna* and the valley of the cave in *Walīd Mas'ūd*[53]), we find illustrations of his dual role as novelist and critic in analyses of literary works (Dostoevsky and Kafka in *al-Safīna*, for example) and in the complex and brilliant taped message which Walīd Mas'ūd leaves behind to tantalise his friends, a piece of writing reminiscent in its language structure of Molly Bloom's soliloquy in Joyce's *Ulysses*.[54] In an article on "The Arabic novel and the major topic", Jabrā suggests that every great novel should operate on two levels, the realistic and the mythic, and that the success of the author can be gauged by the extent to which he is able to fuse the two levels together convincingly.[55] The use of myth has certainly been a major feature of much modern literature, be it Ulysses, Sisyphus, the Phoenix, Adonis or Sindbad. In accordance with his own dictum, Jabrā has supplied a mythic dimension to much of his fiction, from the voyage at sea in a search for consolation from the agonies of exile to a futile search for meaning in a world which keeps saying, in Ṣāyigh's words, "No entry". Jabrā's novels concerning the Palestinian question are among the most sophisticated and technically assured in the modern tradition.

Abdallah Laroui notes in his discussion of the Arab intellectual that the Palestine question is "the Arab problem par excellence", a view to which Jabrā also subscribes.[56] The fact that in the preceding pages we have been able to mention works by novelists from Morocco, Lebanon and Iraq as well as Palestine itself gives ample proof of the widespread concern over the fate of the Palestinians and the manifold ramifications of the issue throughout the Arab world. On the literary plane as well as the political, it is an obvious, perhaps the most obvious, focus of commitment among the Arab intelligentsia. For that

[53] *al-Safīna*, Beirut: Dār al-Ādāb, 1979, 5, 147 ff.; *al-Baḥth 'an Walīd Mas'ūd*, Beirut: Dār al-Ādāb, 1978, 113-33.

[54] *Ibid.*, 26-34.

[55] Jabrā, *al-Riḥla al-thāmina*, Sidon and Beirut: al-Maktaba al-'Aṣriyya, 1967, 105.

[56] *The crisis of the Arab intellectual*, 171. Jabrā, *op. cit.*, 103.

reason, we have considered it first and in some detail. The confrontation with Israel is, of course, one, albeit conspicuous, aspect of a larger issue, the confluence and clash of the cultures of East and West, which in turn leads on the political level to such topics as opposition to European imperial domination, nationalist movements and the struggle for independence, and on the social plane to an examination of the processes of revolution and the impact of societal change. The modern Arabic novel, that genre which can show, in Trilling's words, "the extent of human variety and the value of this variety", has addressed itself to these issues as they have affected the different countries of the Arab world, each one with its particular set of local circumstances. The result is a tradition of diversity and richness, and we will now examine some of its salient features in detail.

It will be recalled that Tawfīq Yūsuf 'Awwād's novel, *al-Raghīf* (discussed above), took as its theme the nationalist struggle during the First World War. In Ḥannā Mīna's novel, *al-Maṣābīḥ al-zurq* ("Blue lamps", 1954), the same struggle is in progress, although the time frame is now the Second World War and the enemy is the French. This work appeared during a decade when the notion of commitment was very much to the fore, and it suffers a good deal because the political message is allowed to predominate over the presentation of characters and events. In fact, the ending of the novel follows the tradition of the romantic novel, with the heroine Randa dying of tuberculosis, while her beloved, Fāris, the freedom-fighter who has joined the army in order to earn enough money to get married, is killed fighting in Libya. The echo of Haykal's *Zaynab* of many decades earlier seems particularly strong. Mīna's second novel, *al-Shirā' wa-al-'āṣifa* ("The sail and the storm", 1966), is a much more accomplished work. As in Ḥalīm Barakāt's *'Awdat al-ṭā'ir ilā al-baḥr* set during the 1967 defeat, we are here dealing with the return to the sea, but in the case of Mīna's novel it is not a condemnation to a continuing exile but rather an aspiration on the hero's part to rejoin the element in which he feels most at home, a theme which several critics have connected with Hemingway's *The old man and the sea*.[57] Al-Ṭurūsī, the major

[57] Ghālī Shukrī, *al-Riwāya al-'Arabiyya fī riḥlat al-'adhāb*, Cairo: 'Ālam al-Kutub, 1971, 235; Sālim, *al-Mughāmara al-riwā'iyya*, 94. For a treatment of this novel as well as a survey of the earlier tradition of the Syrian novel, see

character of this work, has lost his ship at sea and opened a café in the Syrian town of Lādhiqiyya or Lattakia, a community wracked by civil unrest and nationalist activity. For him, this period on land is a time of alienation, but it is also a time during which he becomes aware of the injustices suffered by his fellow-men, the porters and dockers in the harbour who have to carry prodigious loads under the merciless scrutiny of the local racketeers and their thugs. In a brutal fight, al-Ṭurūsī defeats one of these thugs and thus symbolically confronts the social injustices of his homeland. The café now becomes an even greater focus for the activity of the local nationalist groups. Al-Ṭurūsī even goes into the business of smuggling arms to resistance groups. But the event which acts as the catalyst for his exile on land is a violent storm in which he rescues another sailor, al-Raḥūmī, from his sinking boat. After many years of alienation, the hero is now given the opportunity to return to his natural environment, the sea, where the turbulence and unpredictability reflect the societal conditions on land which he has worked so hard to combat and defeat. This novel and others by Mīna take as their theme the quest for freedom on the part of his fellow-countrymen. In the earlier works this tends to be an external quest: freedom from oppression, colonial rule and exploitation, whereas in more recent works the quest has involved more internal factors, release from the burdens of the heritage of the past and from the feelings of alienation of the present. In all this, Mīna has continued to use a vivid realism which makes no concessions to such devices as flashback or stream-of-consciousness in order to recall the past. The narrative sequence is uncomplicated and the impact is often similar to the heroic saga, something to which even more emphasis is given in *al-Shirāʿ wa-al-ʿāṣifa* by the way in which the major character is presented. Mīna states his views on this subject clearly:

> I must admit that, for me, realism should not avoid romanticism nor adopt it totally. Instead, it should make use of romanticism along with all the other literary schools for the purpose of its own particular creative vision. Realism is broad enough to encompass a mixture of a

ʿAdnān ibn Dhurayl, *al-Riwāya al-ʿArabiyya al-Sūriyya*, Damascus: n.p., 1973, esp. 162 ff.; and Ḥusām al-Khaṭīb, *al-Riwāya al-Sūriyya fī marḥalat al-nuhūḍ*, Cairo: al-Munaẓẓama al-ʿArabiyya li-al-Tarbiya wa-al-Thaqāfa wa-al-ʿUlūm, 1975.

number of hues, but it still remains the vehicle whereby all the different hues blend together.[58]

This theme of the struggle for independence is particularly prevalent in fictional works written by novelists in the Maghrib. In ʿAbd al-Karīm Ghallāb's work, *Dafannā al-māḍī* ("We have buried the past", 1966), the scene is set in Fez, that most traditional of Moroccan cities. The family of al-Ḥājj Muḥammad is a microcosm revealing all the latent tensions of a nation under foreign domination which are reflected in the different personalities of the children of the family. While ʿAbd al-Ghanī, the eldest son, opens a shop in the market, ʿAbd al-Raḥmān goes to the secular *madrasa* (school) and becomes involved in nationalist activities which lead inevitably to his imprisonment for long periods and to a sense of shame and resignation in his traditionalist father. Maḥmūd, the son who results from al-Ḥājj Muḥammad's purchase of the slavegirl, Yasmīn, becomes a member of the judiciary responsible for sentencing nationalist trouble-makers like his own half-brother, ʿAbd al-Raḥmān. If this brief description of the characters and their functions within the plot seems somewhat trite, then that indeed reflects the overall impact of the novel. In a rather pretentious introduction, the author informs us that this work is a "committed novel", and indeed, it displays many of the faults which can often be attributed to an excessively close involvement on the author's part in the action of the work itself. Many chapters are filled with sermonettes of varying length in which the characters discuss current societal issues: the education of women, modernism versus traditionalism, loyalty to the homeland, and so on. This close involvement of the author in his work of fiction is carried even further in *Sabʿat abwāb* ("Seven doors", 1965) which, as Muḥammad Mandūr points out, is a graphic description of the author's incarceration without trial for a period of six months for engaging in nationalist activities.[59]

The struggle for national liberation and its aftermath are treated with more subtlety in the works of the Algerian novelist, al-Ṭāhir Waṭṭār, and no more so than in *al-Zilzāl* ("The earthquake", 1974). The particular focus of this work is agricultural reform, and the author manages to convey post-

[58] *al-Mawqif al-adabī* V/3 (July 1975), 122.

[59] Ghallāb, *Sabʿat abwāb*, Cairo: Dār al-Maʿārif, 1965, 5.

revolutionary attitudes with great clarity and force by using the figure of Shaykh ʿAbd al-Majīd Bū-Arwāḥ, a landowner and teacher who returns to his home town in order to dispose of as much of his land as possible to his heirs before the reform law takes effect. The "earthquake" of the title refers both to the physical transformation of the earth's crust (and the city of Constantine where the novel is set lies on such a fault line), but also refers to a quotation form the Qur'ān (Sūra XXII, 1) which is repeated by the Shaykh throughout the novel. As he makes his disgruntled way around the city, he notices the changes which the revolution has brought about and discovers to his dismay that all his descendants to whom he is hoping to bequeath his land have in one way or another become reconciled to the realities of the revolution. Here, too, there is much discussion of current societal and political issues, but in Waṭṭār's work it is conducted within the framework of the Shaykh's internal monologue as he quotes the text of the Qur'ān, curses Ibn Khaldūn for his theories of civilisation, and hopes for the physical or societal earthquake which will eradicate all the revolutionary changes which have so radically altered his lifestyle and surroundings. This novel represents a most successful manipulation of the narrative point of view, since the achievements of the Algerian revolution attained after a great deal of social upheaval and bloodshed are seen through the eyes of a character whose attitude is totally antagonistic.

Algeria gained her independence after a protracted and bloody conflict. In the case of Iraq, while there was no actual fighting on the scale of the Algerian conflict, the decade which preceded the 1958 overthrow of the Iraqi monarchy was one of political instability and social unrest. Ghā'ib Ṭuʿma Farmān's novel, *Khamsat aṣwāt* ("Five voices", 1967), provides a realistic picture of those times as seen through the eyes of five characters drawn from the intellectual, bourgeois class. The author assigns a number from one to five to each character and then introduces them in turn. The first is Saʿīd, a young man in his twenties who works on the complaints column of the newspaper *al-Nās*. The second is Ibrāhīm, the editor-in-chief to the newspaper. Through these two characters and their profession the reader is introduced to a wide variety of social and political issues; indeed, their livelihood is frequently threatened by "suggestions", "recommendations", and even orders from the censors, while at the conclusion of the work the newspaper is closed down altogether.[60] In this way, the social tensions which existed during Nūrī Saʿīd's tutelage of the Iraqi governmental apparatus before the revolution are clearly illustrated. The other three "voices" are, in turn, ʿAbd al-Khāliq, Sharīf, a would-be poet and philanderer, and lastly Ḥāmid, a senior bank official. The frequent meetings between these five characters in bars, restaurants, buses and so on, allow for discussions of a wide variety of topics of local and international interest: Palestine, the Arab League, Guatemala; the alienation of intellectuals, the virtues of city and provincial living, the rights of women. Indeed, this aspiration for a realistic setting and treatment is often carried too far, as for example when Saʿīd retraces his steps back to the places of his youth in an extended passage.[61] The novel does however have a central focus to its plot. Saʿīd receives an anonymous letter at his office concerning the plight of a housewife who is being maltreated by her husband. Research reveals that the husband is none other than Ḥāmid himself, something which causes considerable embarrassment to the entire group. Eventually Ḥalīma, Ḥāmid's wife (or Najāt, as she is called in the initial letter to Saʿīd), returns to her home town of Karbalā'. At the end of the work, Ḥāmid has been rejected by the girl at the bank with whom he has been flirting throughout the sorry episode with his wife, and Sharīf the poet has been thrown out by his prostitute girl friend, Ṣabriyya. According to the canons of social realism, we are to assume that the opportunists and philanderers have been given their just deserts. With the closing of the newspaper, Saʿīd takes that decision adopted by so many young Arab intellectuals who find themselves at odds with the authorities, namely to leave the country, and the work ends with him saying farewell to his father.

A particularly interesting aspect of this novel is its narrative technique. The majority of chapters deal with one of the five characters, but on two occasions the canvas expands to incorporate all five at once. The narrative throughout is told in the third person, so that the portrait of each individual remains more external than is the case in, for example, Maḥfūẓ's *Mīrāmār* or Jabrā's *al-Safīna*, other examples of what Ḍiyā' al-

[60] *Khamsat aṣwāt*, Beirut: Dār al-Ādāb, 1967, 22, 49, 63, 287.
[61] *Ibid.*, 238 ff.

Sharqāwī terms *riwāyāt ṣawtiyya*.[62] However, even if Farmān does not exploit the potentialities of the "novel of voices" to the full, his novel is a convincing portrait of Iraqi society at a crucial period in its modern history, and the final chapter in which the five voices are merged depicts that tantalising mixture of despair and hope which characterised the period immediately prior to the revolution of 1958.

Accounts of life in Iraq after 1958 suggest that one tyranny was replaced by another, in the form of the régime of 'Abd al-Karīm Qāsim, who was to be overthrown in 1963 by yet another bloody revolution. The atmosphere of those early days of the Iraqi Revolution is well captured by Ismā'īl Fahd Ismā'īl in his quartet of novels which will be discussed in detail in the next chapter. For one of the characters in that work, the very name Qāsim is one which haunts his entire life. Having written a poem against the country's ruler, he is first imprisoned without trial or charge, then found to have no links with any of the banned political organisations, and finally prevented from obtaining any kind of employment because he is now for ever labelled as "a dangerous political extremist".

The works which we have just discussed and many others like them serve to illustrate the way in which the Arabic novel has been used to describe and even prescribe the processes of political and social change in the Arab world since the Second World War. Some of the novels have dealt with the circumstances which led to the revolution, as in the works of Maḥfūẓ and Farmān, while others have discussed the aftermath, as in the works of Ismā'īl and Waṭṭār. Waṭṭār's novel, *al-Zilzāl*, it will be remembered, treats the issues of agricultural reform from within the context of the city, and the attitudes of the main character to people living in the countryside find many echoes in other works: al-Ḥājj Muḥammad in Ghallāb's *Dafannā al-māḍī* and Sharīf and Ḥāmid in *Khamsat aṣwāt* by Farmān all reflect the supercilious and often exploitative views of the urban bourgeoisie.[63] This theme can be traced back to the beginnings of modern Arabic fiction; the *'umda* in al-Muwayliḥī's *Ḥadīth 'Īsā ibn Hishām* and Ḥāmid in Haykal's *Zaynab* serve as vehicles for the discussion of this issue. With this in mind, we may

[62] al-Sharqāwī, "al-Mi'mār al-fannī fī riwāyat al-Safīna", *al-Ma'rifa* 193-4 (March-April 1978), 7-57.

[63] See, for example, *Khamsat aṣwāt*, 16.

observe that these authors seem to reflect Lionel Trilling's opinion with regard to the Western novel that

Few of our novelists are able to write about the poor so as to make them something more than the pitied objects of our facile sociological minds.[64]

However, while Trilling's comment may apply to the Arabic novel in quantitative terms, there are a significant number of works of fiction which deal with the lives of poor people in both the city and the countryside. On the latter topic, the Egyptian tradition is particularly rich, and the distinguished critic ʿAbd al-Muḥsin Ṭāhā Badr has devoted an entire book to the subject, *al-Riwāʾī wa-al-arḍ* ("The novelist and the earth", 1971). Within the context of agricultural reform, the name of ʿAbd al-Raḥmān al-Sharqāwī immediately springs to mind, in that his novel, *al-Arḍ* ("The earth". 1954; translated as *Egyptian earth*[65]), was in the view of many commentators one of the strongest advocates of the agricultural reform measures which were introduced in the early days of the Egyptian Revolution. While the work is set in the tyrannical régime of Ismāʿīl Ṣidqī in the 1930s, the contemporary import of the novel was not lost on anyone; indeed, one of the criticisms of the work may be that the message is too obtrusive at times. Set in an Egyptian village beset by all the problems and injustices of an inequitable system of water distribution and of a corrupt local and provincial authority structure, this novel provides cogent evidence of the need for agricultural reform. The focus of the village's opposition is a new road which the authorities plan to build through the peasants' land to the house of the local Pāshā, but within that structure the reader is introduced to a whole series of authentically-alive Egyptian peasant characters, from Waṣīfa, the earthy and sharp-tongued village beauty, to ʿAlwānī, the wily and feckless Bedouin, from Shaykh Shinnāwī, the village teacher and *muftī*, to ʿAbd al-Hādī, the industrious farmer and one of several men who are in love with Waṣīfa. Al-Sharqāwī succeeds brilliantly in conveying the daily life, squabbles, loves and intrigues of this set of characters. His use of the colloquial language in the dialogue is particularly effective in conveying to the reader the earthy humour of these peasants as they struggle

64 *The liberal imagination*, 87.
65 By Desmond Stewart, Delhi: Hind Pocket Books, 1972.

in a bitter-sweet existence to combat the combined vicissitudes of nature and corruption.[66]

Al-Sharqāwī's commitment to the cause of social reform is at times obtrusive in *al-Arḍ*; some of the authority figures in particular seem to be two-dimensional. Even so, the depiction of village characters in an authentic setting is handled with great skill. Another of al-Sharqāwī's novels, *al-Fallāḥ* ("The peasant", 1967), is also set in an Egyptian village, but during the revolutionary period. The work aims to show that, while the advent of the revolution has brought about some changes in provincial living, and especially in education, the old feudal authority system has been replaced by an equally monolithic structure, that of the Arab Socialist Union which is quite as talented at obfuscation and outright deceit as anything which the *ancien régime* could produce.

Another writer who has concerned himself with the life of the poor in both city and countryside is Yūsuf Idrīs. The less salubrious areas of Cairo form the backdrop to many of his short stories, and to them he brings his personal experiences as a medical inspector. Examples range from the short vignette *Naẓra* ("A stare", from *Arkhaṣ layālī*, 1954), to the sizeable novella *Qā' al-madīna* ("City dregs", 1957).[67] The short story *Mishwār* ("A trip" from *Arkhaṣ layālī*) is an effective combination of provincial attitudes to the big city and city reactions to country yokels. Another short story, *Ḥādithat sharaf* ("An affair of honour" from the collection of that name, 1958) is a brilliant portrayal of the fish-bowl society on a country estate, and may be considered as a precedent for what I regard as his best novel, *al-Ḥarām* ("The taboo", 1959). In this work, Idrīs paints a wonderfully vivid picture of an Egyptian village wracked by suspicion at the discovery of a discarded newborn baby. To the innate suspicions and grudges of the village itself is added the complication and, from the point of view of plot, fascinating new dimension of the *tarāḥīl* or migrant workers who are, almost automatically, regarded as the culprits. When it is discovered that one of the village women, 'Azīza, is the

[66] See Ṭāhā Badr, *al-Riwā'ī wa-ad-arḍ*, Cairo: al-Hay'a al-Miṣriyya al-'Āmma li-al-Kitāb, 1971, 113-53; Kilpatrick, *The modern Egyptian novel*, 126-33; 'Alī Jād, "'Abd ar-Raḥmān ash-Sharqāwī's *al-Arḍ*", *JAL* VII (1976), 88-100.

[67] Both are translated in *In the eye of the beholder*, ed. Roger Allen, Chicago.: Bibliotheca Islamica, 1978.

mother of the baby and that she has been raped, attitudes change; when she dies, the sadness of the entire affair draws the two antagonistic groups together. The novel ends with a description of the way in which the Agricultural Reform Law brings about changes in the lives of the villagers. This somewhat contrived insertion, along with the "happy ending", tend to detract from the overall impact of the work, but in other aspects Idrīs's novel is most effective.

One area of the provinces of Egypt which is not unfamiliar to people in the West is that of Luxor and Aswan, and in recent times some younger writers have chosen to set their novels in this environment. Yaḥyā al-Ṭāhir ʻAbdallāh was in fact born in al-Karnak, the village just to the north of Luxor, and many of his short stories and his novel, *al-Ṭawq wa-al-aswira* ("The necklet and bracelets", 1975) are set in the Upper Egyptian milieu with which he is so familiar. Ṣanʻallāh Ibrāhīm's *Najmat Aghustus* ("Star of August", n.d.) takes as its theme the building of the High Dam south of Aswan.[68] One of the social problems associated with the environmental impact of the building of this huge structure was the resettlement of the Nubian villagers who were to be displaced by the rising waters of the Nile.[69] With that in mind, it is interesting to note that Fatḥī Ghānim addressed himself to the question of resettlement and the almost inevitable clash of traditional and modernist values in his first novel, *al-Jabal* ("The mountain", 1957). The setting is the West Bank of the Nile opposite Luxor. The government has decided to build a model village for the people of Gurna in the hope of preventing the continued pillaging of the Pharaonic tombs and manufacture of fakes through which the villagers earn their livelihood.[70] For this purpose, an architect has designed and built a modern village with all the most modern conveniences, but the villagers steadfastly refuse to move from the cave dwellings on "the mountain". Threats to move them by force are of no avail in the face of the stalwart opposition of the village *ʻumda* and his community. The lack of sympathy and understanding between the two groups is illustrated in a number of ways, as, for example, in the fact that the architect has designed the houses

[68] See Maḥmūd Amīn al-ʻĀlim, *al-Ādāb* (Feb.-March 1980), 15-20.

[69] See Robert Fernea, *Nubians in Egypt*, Austin: University of Texas Press, 1973, 36-47.

[70] This is also the subject of a very famous Egyptian film entitled *al-Mūmiyā* ("The mummy").

with domed roofs in order to keep the houses cool in the summer heat, whereas to the villagers only tombs are constructed with domes and they have no desire to live in such ill-omened homes.

Fatḥī Ghānim succeeds in placing the events of this novel within a realistic background, but many of the characters involved emerge purely as stereotypes, and especially those whose names are not revealed—the architect, the Princess and the French woman. But perhaps the most serious fault in the work concerns the narrative technique itself. The young investigator who comes from Cairo to write a report on the situation is himself named Fatḥī Ghānim,[71] and indeed there is very little narrative distance between the author of this work and the narrator of the story. Not only is the narrator possessed of an unsubtle omniscience, but also Fatḥī Ghānim the author-narrator allows his moments of contemplation to become something akin to lectures as in the following two examples:

When my eye alighted on the very first page, I felt myself transported to a strange world, far from reality, full of dreams and fancies. This is the kind of thing that we city folk do when confronted with another type of society which is different from the one to which we are used. In our minds we immediately change it into a fancy, a story, a film or a myth. ...
The fake statues they made with their own hands, they were the real treasure, the genuine artefacts. They weren't forgeries. They had made them with their hands and through their own labour. Work, that was the real treasure.[72]

The latter quotation not only shows another problem connected with the question of resettling the villagers—namely, that no-one has thought what work the villagers might do once they are resettled—but also illustrates the change in the narrator's attitude towards the villagers, so much so that he fails to write a report on his visit and is eventually fired from his post.

Al-Jabal thus emerges as an effective portrayal of yet another aspect of the clash between the city and the countryside, the traditional and the modern, but its impact as a work of fiction is lessened by the author's proximity to his narrator. One may perhaps suggest that Ghānim's journalistic profession has

[71] *al-Jabal*, Cairo: Dār al-Hilāl, 1965, 57.
[72] *Ibid.*, 11, 156.

intruded into his function as a novelist. This said, it should be added immediately that his later novel, *al-Rajul alladhī faqada ẓillahu* ("The man who lost his shadow", 1960?) shows a more sophisticated use of narrative technique; indeed, it is regarded as one of the most notable contributions to the emerging tradition of multi-narrator fiction.[73] In the words of Kingsley Amis:

> Mr Ghanem is a careful and conscientious craftsman who has clearly devoted a good deal of thought to the art of the novel ... as a novelist myself, what I most admire is the sheer literary skill with which the material is shaped and handled, the transitions between various moments in time are expertly handled ...[74]

Of the novels depicting life in the countryside which we have considered thus far, it is al-Sharqāwī's *al-Arḍ* which manages to present the liveliest milieu. This is due in no small part, as we noted above, to his ability to convey the humour of the villagers and their willingness to take a sardonically fatalistic attitude to the series of events which often constitute the real purpose of the novel. The Lebanese critic and littérateur Mārūn ʿAbbūd (1866-1962) allows this humorous aspect to come even more to the fore in his novel, *Fāris Āghā* (n.d.), which gives a thoroughly tongue-in-cheek view of a Lebanese village in "an age gone by" (to quote the subtitle) as the inhabitants try to outfox each other and the successive layers of provincial authority during the Ottoman period. It has to be admitted that this is a curious work. While the humour is at first infectious, it is not enough to carry the reader through a work which is lacking in narrative structure. ʿAbbūd makes use of his erudition as one of the Arab world's most illustrious literary critics, even to the extent of making references to classical poets such as Imru' al-Qays, Bashshār and al-Mutanabbī in the text, but the subject matter seems to demand a less erudite treatment than this and the result is tedious and unconvincing.

Palestine, the struggle for national independence, changes in the fabric of society and urbanisation, these are large issues which have almost naturally provided the themes for a number

[73] See Fatma Moussa-Mahmoud, *The Arabic novel in Egypt*, Cairo: General Egyptian Book Organization, 1973, 71-8.

[74] Quoted on the back cover of Desmond Stewart' translation, *The man who lost his shadow*, London: Heinemann, and Washington: Three Continents Press, 1980.

of Arabic novels written during the last three or four decades. Indeed, it is the very choice of these particular subjects which has allowed us to incorporate so many works by authors of different nationalities and techniques in the preceding pages. However, the bulk of these novels has been concerned with the portrayal of groups of people in their struggle with the vicissitudes of life in the Arab world today. As we noticed with regard to the career of Najīb Maḥfūẓ, the period of the late 1950s and 1960s saw an increasing tendency among many Arab novelists to move "into the labyrinth" (to use Sasson Somekh's phrase) by concentrating more on the individual in his societal environment. Reviews in literary magazines contained frequent references to Kafka and Camus. Within the realm of committed literature, this can be seen with particular clarity in the works of Muṭāʿ Ṣafadī. *Thā'ir muḥtarif* ("A professional revolutionary", 1961) concerns a revolutionary who has participated in struggles throughout the Arab world and is looked up to by the younger generation. However, he has grown tired of slogans and the formation of cells and structures. Now he is more interested in the revolt of the individual. As he expresses it, "Revolution isn't a school from which you graduate; first and foremost it is the experience of the hero confronted by himself."[75] Both ʿAbd al-Karīm al-Ashtar and Jabrā Ibrāhīm Jabrā warn in their critical writings about the dangers of excessive commitment in literature: characters behaving "like wind-up dolls" and narrative degenerating into journalism and slogans.[76] While Karīm, the hero of Ṣafadī's novel, announces his dislike of "the sound of the public trumpet," there remains a good deal of reportage in the text which does not emerge naturally from the portrayal or development of character. Other portraits of revolutionary Arab intellectuals are painted with a more subtle artistry.

The novels which we have discussed thus far in this chapter, for all their differences, have one thing in common: they were written by males. That the overwhelming preponderance of novelists in the period we have been discussing have been men is, of course, a comment on societal tradition and particularly education. Alongside the developments which we described in

75 See Shukrī ʿAyyād in *ʿĀlam al-Fikr* III/3 (Oct.-Dec. 1972), 640.

76 See al-Ashtar, *Dirāsa fī adab al-nakba*, 6-7; Jabrā, in *al-Ḥurriyya wa-al-ṭūfān*, 18-22.

earlier chapters another process has been going on, one which in the minds of many Middle Eastern women is by no means complete, namely the improvement of women's status. In the present context, that includes the freedom to express themselves in novels with the realism and frankness which the genre demands. Najīb Maḥfūẓ is able to put the process into a historical context in his *al-Marāyā* ("Mirrors", 1972):

The girl students in 1930 were very few in number, no more then ten altogether. They all had the stamp of the harem about them. They dressed modestly, wore no earrings or bracelets, and sat together in the front row of the lecture hall, as though they were in the women's section of a tramcar. At first we neither greeted them nor talked to them. If we absolutely had to ask a question or borrow a notebook, then the whole thing was done with a cautious shyness. However, this did not continue peaceably for long. They soon started to attract attention.[77]

As the author makes clear, this stage was just the beginning of the process. Conservative societal attitudes are well captured in Maḥfūẓ's *Bayn al-qaṣrayn*, the first volume of *The trilogy*, in which ʿAbd al-Jawwād throws his wife out of the house for disobeying his instructions not to go out.[78] Another aspect of woman's position in society is conveyed by Laṭīfa al-Zayyāt in her novel *al-Bāb al-maftūḥ* ("The open door", 1960):

When a girl is born, they all give a smile of resignation. When she grows up, they put her in a prison and train her in the art of living, to smile, to curtsy, to put on perfume and look delicate, to dissimulate, to wear a corset, and to get married. To whom, you ask? Any man. All you have to worry about is his money. The woman had better be greedy for love, very greedy ... but there should be no feelings, sentiment, thought or love shown in public or else they'll kill her ...[79]

The resentment felt by many women at their status in society is explicit enough in this extract, but it is expressed with even greater defiance in the writings of Laylā Baʿalbakkī and Colette Khūrī. The earlier works of these novelists earned them both fame and even notoriety and stimulated a number of adulatory and severely critical reviews, few of which concentrated on the

[77] 160; trans. Allen, 106.

[78] The section is translated in E.W. Fernea and B.Q. Bezirgan, *Middle Eastern Muslim women speak*, Austin: University of Texas Press, 1977, 95-123.

[79] Quoted in Fu'ād Duwwāra, *Fī al-riwāya al-Miṣriyya*, Cairo: Dār al-Kātib al-ʿArabī, n.d., 152.

literary qualities of the works themselves. This tendency was carried even further when Laylā Baʿalbakkī was arrested in 1964 for offending public morality through her short story, *Safīnat ḥinān ilā al-qamar* ("Spaceship of tenderness to the moon")[80] The works of these two writers were by women and about women, a mixture already explosive enough for conservative circles, but the point was made even stronger by the fact that both make use of the first-person narrative mode, thus lending a convincing proximity to the relationship between the writer and the speaker. Colette Khūrī's novel, *Ayyām maʿahu* ("Days with him"), was an instant *cause célèbre* because of its frank description of a love affair between a young girl and an older man whom she eventually rejects, but it became even more so when rumour had it that the "him" of the title was none other than Nizār Qabbānī, the Arab world's most famous poet who had made the cause of women in Arab society one of the major themes of his earlier poetry. Laylā Baʿalbakkī's second novel, *al-Āliha al-mamsūkha* ("Deformed Deities", 1960), also concerns a love affair between a young girl and a middle-aged man, but in this novel and her first and more famous work, *Anā aḥyā* ("I am alive", 1958), the primary focus is on the position of the girl within the family and her view of herself. The opinions of Līna, the heroine of the latter work, about her father's house are encapsulated in the final paragraph of the novel:

So I went home again. It's as though I was forced to do it. I always have to go home; to eat at home, to sleep, to bathe. My entire destiny seems to be tied up in this home.[81]

To Khālida Saʿīd, the distinguished Lebanese critic and wife of the poet Adūnīs, this novel was "a *cri de coeur* which protested not only against the enslavement of women but also against the female syndrome, woman-wife-mother, which restricted her entire existence to the level of biological functions."[82] And yet, while there can be no doubt about the writer's commitment to

80 For a translation of the story and transcript of the trial, see Fernea and Bezirgan, *op. cit.*, 271-90. The translation (by Denys Johnson-Davies) is to be found in *Modern Arabic short stories*, London: Heinemann, and Washington: Three Continents Press, 1976, 126-34.

81 *Anā aḥyā*, Beirut: Dār Majallat Shiʿr, 1963, 317.

82 "al-Riwāya al-ʿArabiyya bayn 1920-1972", *Mawāqif* 28 (Summer 1974), 82.

change, the overall effect is not a little narcissistic. As Ḥalīm Barakāt notes:

> The defiant mood of Līna—the protagonist of Laylā Baʿalbakkī in her novel *Anā Aḥyā (I live)*—is deeply rooted in her egotistic assertion of her individual freedom. Her strong feelings and ideas spring from a point of view which focuses on her ego to the almost total exclusion of social reality. What is at issue for her is her personal problems.[83]

This predominance of the personal is underlined by the extreme prolixity of the work. The second novel, *al-Āliha al-mamsūkha*, shows a greater control of the narrative structure, but the characters in both works remain somewhat two-dimensional.

Another female novelist from Lebanon is Emily Naṣrallāh, who shares with Baʿalbakkī and Khūrī a concern for the status of women but whose choice of theme and mood is completely different. Indeed her prize-winnning novel, *Ṭuyūr Aylūl* ("September birds", 1962), manages to combine several of the themes which we have been considering during the course of this chapter: the fate of women within the traditional societal system, the contrast between life in the city and the village, and contact with the West and in particular emigration. The very title of the work, with its romantic associations with nature, recalls the fictional works of Jubrān. As in *al-Arwāḥ al-mutamarrida* ("Spirits rebellious") of many years earlier, the countryside of Lebanon and its natural phenomena are used as the backdrop for a work of social criticism, although, in Naṣrallāh's case, the homiletic element so obtrusive in Jubrān's works is entirely absent and the message is allowed to emerge from the events themselves. The narrator, a village girl who has moved to the city, looks back on her childhood and adolescence in the traditional society of her native village. The environment combines a proximity to nature and its accompanying beauty with all the gossip, scandal, ritualised joy and tragedy of a tightly-knit, fishbowl society. Along with the narrator's sense of alienation from and longing for this microcosm, there emerge the tragedies of a number of young people raised in the village who are imprisoned within the web of idle chatter and arranged marriages concocted for them by their elders. Some of them manage to escape the inevitable by emigrating to the United States. Others find refuge in death, and still others resign

[83] *Visions of social reality in the contemporary Arab novel*, 23-4.

themselves to the inevitable dictates of this traditional society. The description of the way in which the village gives the cold shoulder to the narrator upon her return to the village on a visit from the city and of the effect on an aged father of young Rājī's departure for the United States remain in the mind as vivid examples of the consequences of societal attitudes as portrayed in this novel. The condemnation implicit in the events of the narrative is made even more forceful in its impact by contrast with the description of the village itself and its environs, something which is achieved in a language of extreme poetic sensitivity.[84]

3. *The writer, the medium and the reader*

In adopting a thematic approach to this survey of the Arabic novel in recent decades, our aim has been to broach some of the major issues which have concerned novelists outside the purely national context often adopted by so many studies of the genre in both Arabic and European languages. Within such a framework, the emphasis has been mainly on extrinsic analysis (to use Wellek and Warren's terminology). There have been some comments of a critical nature, but the more intrinsic approach to the Arabic novel as a literary text is taken up in the next chapter in which eight novels (to which some reference has already been made in previous chapters) are analysed as individual contributions to the genre. Still within the context of the present chapter, however, it should be noted that our treatment thus far has dealt primarily with the novels themselves, or, in other works, with the text. Much modern literary analysis places the text and its "speaker" within the framework of a communicative act between the writer on the one hand and the reader on the other. In concluding this chapter, it seems appropriate to consider briefly those particular features which mark this process of communication within the context of the Arabic novel.

In an article about reality and realism in the Arabic novel, the Maghribi writer, Mubārak Rabīʿ, assesses the posture of the novelist in these terms:

> At the moment our daily reality represents a bitter crisis on all levels and with no dissimulation. All this would seem to justify our posture of questioning, argument, criticism, review and evaluation of every-

[84] *Ṭuyūr Aylūl*, Beirut: Mu'assasat Nawfal, 1977, 124, 243 ff.

thing which comes within our purview, both within us and outside us.[85]

This gloomy view of the reality which the Arab novelist is called upon to portray has been reflected in many of the works discussed in this chapter; to quote Lukacs, it is indeed "a world that has been abandoned by God."[86] In the preceding pages we have seen several examples of what Farīda al-Naqqāsh describes:

> ... prisons and torture, police chases and a constricting surveillance, exile, tunnels and deserts, death by martyrdom and death instead of others, emigration away from the homeland and into the realm of the self, thousands of masks—false names and hideaways—and compulsory banishment from the real source, the masses at large.[87]

She is basing her comments on a series of novels drawn from the Arab world as a whole, from al-Ṭāhir Waṭṭār in the West via Najīb Maḥfūẓ and Jamāl al-Ghīṭānī in Egypt to ʿAbd al-Raḥmān Munīf in Iraq. From our own sample we can cite the experiences of heroes in works by Ismāʿīl Fahd Ismāʿīl and Jabrā Ibrāhīm Jabrā as examples of the fate of writers who traverse the thin line established by the régimes in various Arab countries in order to suppress "questioning, argument and criticism" which might become too adventurous. And, while the accounts in the novels themselves will often reflect personal experience, we do not need to rely on fictional works in order to document the often risky situations into which Arab novelists have placed themselves in fulfilling their role as commentators on and critics of society. Fact can tell us that ʿAbd al-Karīm Ghallāb, Yūsuf Idrīs, and Ṣanʿallāh Ibrāhīm (among others) have all spent time in prison and/or exile, Ḥalīm Barakāt was dismissed from his teaching position at a Lebanese University and Laylā Baʿalkakkī was subjected to arrest and trial.[88] Not that a work of literature was involved in every case, but all these writers were evaluating "everything which comes within their purview" in one way of another. We have cited these littérateurs as contributors to fiction; if the other literary genres were to be included, the catalogue of imprisonment, torture,

[85] *al-Ādāb* (Feb.-Mar. 1980), 29.
[86] *The theory of the novel*, 88.
[87] *al-Ādāb* (Feb.-March 1980), 33.
[88] The experiences of Ṣanʿallāh Ibrāhīm and ʿAbd al-Karīm Ghallāb are described in *ibid.*, 100-3, 115-20.

exile, harassment and censorship could be greatly extended. Novelists in the Arab world are, needless to say, not the only ones who have suffered under such conditions; the careers of Pasternak and Solzhenitsyn within the Soviet Union provide their own evidence, nor is the record of many Western countries entirely clean on the matter of censorship of literature. However, it seems accurate to suggest that, in carrying out their function as surveyors and critics of society, Arab novelists have often needed courage as well as commitment and have paid dearly for any miscalculations of the prevailing attitudes of the cultural establishment. The alternative to such a stance has often been quiescence and/or exile, and, as Jabrā has observed with regard to the modern Arab littérateur:

> If he does not rebel and defend his individual entity, he will lose ... his identity and in the name of humanity, progress or freedom ... the ideologists will exploit his powers. Then all that distinguishes him, his special vision of life, his understanding of history or his sympathy for humanity will be obliterated.[89]

Another novelist, Suhayl Idrīs, the editor of *al-Ādāb* which, as we noted earlier, has since its foundation been in the forefront of the advocacy of committed literature in the modern Arab world, allows himself to finish a statement on his personal career as a novelist with a *cri de cœur*, aptly summarising the unfortunate realities which we have just outlined; it is thus worth quoting *in extenso*:

> This crisis is one of freedom of expression. Can the Arab writer always stand up and challenge it? Doesn't such a challenge often subject him to pressures, constraints on his livelihood, and a variety of kinds of oppression and terror? ... What is he supposed to say about other people in the dreadful atmosphere of decline in which the Arab nation finds itself today? Shouldn't he condemn the prevailing authority structures and foundations, and impute to them all the causes of this decline? Is he not to be allowed to say what he wants? Where can he find the sphere in which to express this challenge if all the modes of information are in the hands of the official organisations and financed by them? Even if there were to be independent information agencies, would they not be permanently threatened with closure if the official organisations were able to deprive their readership of what they read?[90]

[89] In *al-Ḥurriyya wa-al-ṭūfān*, 22-3, as quoted in al-Jayyusi, *Trends and movements in modern Arabic poetry*, II, 582-3.

[90] *al-Ādāb* (Feb.-March 1980), 99.

The mention of publication in Idrīs's remarks permits us to move from some of the more unsubtle realities faced by novelists in the Arab world to more subtle ones. Novel writing, to ʿAbd al-Nabī Ḥijāzī, is a confrontation with "the self, society and the authorities," and no more so than in the area of publication; for "the novel is a book, and books are a commodity exposed to a continuous chain of censorship, printing and marketing operations. It is these factors which force the novelist to back down sometimes, albeit bitterly and regretfully".[91]

Nor do these constraints mark the only ways through which novelists find themselves frustratingly beholden to the authorities in their countries. Writing fiction is not and never has been a profession by which even the most famous writers such as Maḥfūẓ can earn a living. Many countries in the region have only recently signed any kind of copyright convention which has international recognition, and sums paid to writers upon receipt of their manuscripts have been extremely small by Western standards. As noted above, the cinema has often provided a fatally-attractive alternative. As one kind of solution to this situation, many writers have found employment within the information network itself, thus becoming a part of the very cultural bureaucracy which surveys fictional production. Indeed, editorships and other posts in literary magazines and other kinds of cultural periodical have allowed a number of writers a certain amount of time to devote their attentions to creative writing, certainly more time than they would otherwise have had if their employment had been in some other sector. The year 1980 continues to find novelists employed in this way: Suhayl Idrīs can wistfully complain about being diverted from creative writing by his editorial functions at *al-Ādāb* itself.[92] ʿAbd al-Raḥmān Munīf serves as editor of the petroleum journal, *al-Nafṭ wa-al-tanmiya* ("Oil and development") published in Baghdad, and in an interview he complains about the relatively small number of novels in Arabic, citing as the cause:

> that there is neither the opportunity nor the time to concentrate completely on writing novels, ... the novel being a complex structure which needs both time and continuous work without interruption ...[93]

[91] *Ibid.*, 53.
[92] *Ibid.*, 98.
[93] *al-Maʿrifa* 204 (Feb. 1979), 189.

A survey of the Egyptian novel in the 1960s undertaken by Sabri Hafez illustrates some of the consequences of this situation.[94] The majority of novelists discussed managed to produce one, or at the most, two novels. In a telling montage, the editors of the Egyption magazine *al-Ṭalīʿa* asked the younger generation of writers to give details of their way of life, job, salary and so on. This is the generation described by Hafez as being

> debarred from all political activity, surrounded with a potent and deceptive propaganda, brought up on a diet of illusive slogans and statements, and asked to sacrifice its freedom for a fragile and corrupt establishment.

While a few of these writers did have junior positions within the cultural sector, many others were employed in positions far removed from literature and the arts, and a few were unemployed.[95]

Returning then to the terminology with which we began this section, we may say that the creator of the novel in the Arab world—as a process of communication between the writer and the reader—often finds himself a controversial member of society, a posture which may have significant effects on his own livelihood. The descriptions on the previous pages illustrate the considerable differences between the life styles of novelists in the Arab world and in most Western countries. And yet, the basic posture of challenge, of confrontation, and of experimentation with "the novel", are, as we have suggested before, intrinsic features of the genre. In Lukacs's words

> The novel tells of the adventure of interiority; the content of the novel is the story of the soul that goes to find itself, that seeks adventures in order to be proved and tested by them, and, by proving itself, to find its own essence.[96]

The other participant in this act of communication is the reader, but before we consider the question of readership in the Arab world, we should discuss the medium through which writer and reader come into contact, namely language. This subject has been responsible for some of the liveliest and longest debates in the history of modern Arabic literature, and indeed they still continue. At the most basic level, we can point to the

[94] "The Egyptian novel in the sixties", 76-7.
[95] See *al-Ṭalīʿa* (Sept. 1969).
[96] *Op. cit.*, 89.

issues associated with the programme of *ta'rīb* (arabisation) in the countries of the Maghrib. During the colonial period, when French had been the predominant language of culture among intellectuals, Arabic had been preserved within the essentially traditional and conservative environment of Islam and its institutions such as the mosque and the Qur'ān school (as 'Abd al-Karīm Ghallāb's novel, *Dafannā al-māḍī*, discussed above, clearly shows). After independence, the countries of the Maghrib sought to rid themselves of vestiges of the French occupation of their countries and to find new political alignments. In Algeria, the new republic has been trying with varying degrees of success to arabise means of communication, but that it has not been easy from a social and political point of view is made clear in a short article in *al-Ādāb* where, within the space of a few lines, we can read the following comments:

> The Algerian people should regard the Arabs as the raiders of North Africa and should deal with Arab culture just as they would with the culture of any other enemy ... By virtue of Algeria's "empathy" with the Mediterranean region, it makes more sense to deal with the countries of the area—France, Italy and Spain—rather than the Arabs of the Arabian Peninsula whose culture and technological progress is still backward.[97]

These views are, needless to say, somewhat extreme, but they are cited in order to demonstrate the complexities of the problem of language usage which faces writers in the countries of the Maghrib. While many, if not most, still write in French, the number of Arabic novels is steadily increasing, and a younger generation of novelists in emerging to take over from the earlier pioneers in the genre whose works, measured by the yardstick of the Arabic novel as a whole, were rather conservative in both themes and techniques.[98]

Another question of language usage is that of the old argument concerning the colloquial and written forms of Arabic. With reference to the novel, the major concern is with the use of the language of speech (the colloquial dialect) in the dialogue. The issue has been discussed vehemently with reference to all literary genres which have a share of the dramatic, and there exists a host of intermediate opinions and solutions

[97] 'Abd al-'Alī Razzāqī, "al-Ta'rīb fī al-Jazā'ir", *al-Ādāb* (June 1980), 73.

[98] See Muḥammad 'Izz al-Dīn al-Tāzī in *al-Ādāb* (Fed.-March 1980), 78-82.

between outright rejection and acceptance. Many Egyptian novelists, for example, have written their dialogue in the colloquial dialect of Cairo or other areas of Egypt (see, for example, Fatḥī Ghānim's *al-Jabal*), believing, no doubt, that both television and films have helped to make these colloquials widely understood throughout the Arab world; this trend goes back to Haykal's *Zaynab* written in 1911. Najīb Maḥfūẓ, on the other hand, does not use the colloquial dialect in the dialogues of his works, although he will occasionally slip in a dialect word or even use colloquial word order, consciously or unconsciously. Many other novelists prefer to compose their entire novel in the written language, basing their decision, no doubt, on aesthetic grounds or else on a desire to obtain a wide readership throughout the Arab world. The considerable complexity of the issue is summarised by Vial in what he admits is a "risky generalisation":

> the tendency to use the spoken "popular" language is more widespread in countries where the literary public is greatest and which believe, rightly or wrongly, that they have a better established "Arab" character—thus in Egypt, rather than Algeria.[99]

The linguistic, social, religious and political ramifications of the issues of language are both plentiful and complex, and in the context of this chapter we have only been able to touch briefly on two. However, the impact of these questions of language on the wider issue of readership has emerged clearly enough, both from the point of view of those who are addressed in particular novels and also those who are, consciously or unconsciously, excluded. In turning to the issue of the readership of the Arabic novel *per se*, we immediately face some other practicalities. The most obvious of these concerns the level of literacy. While little, if any, statistically valid data exist on this subject within the Arab world, it seems reasonable to suggest that the percentage

[99] *EI*[2] art. "Ḳiṣṣa". As an aside, I must say that Vial's expressed belief that the word *qiṣṣa* is becoming accepted as the standard word for "novel" seems to me completely wrong. A quick reference to the bibliography of this volume will show clearly that numerous writers have written separate works on both the short story and novel genres (ʿAdnān ibn Dhurayl, Yūsuf ʿIzz al-Dīn, and Aḥmad Haykal are just three examples from different parts of the Arab world), and to all of them the word *qiṣṣa* means "story", and the word *riwāya* means "novel". One must hope that, when in the fullness of time, *EI*[2] reaches the letter R, it will be possible to update Vial's otherwise excellent survey and at the same time devote the "Ḳiṣṣa" entry to the shorter genre.

of literate readers in those countries where Arabic novels are published is substantially lower (as a percentage of the total population) than is the case in Western countries. Furthermore, the percentage of readers in the West who regularly read novels is also small. As Q.D. Leavis has noted in her pioneering study of the readership of fiction, novels demand of the reader time, motivation and intelligence, and contemporary life offers a large number of temptations in the form of less demanding and more accessible art forms.[100] Within the context of the Arab world, we are dealing then with a relatively small percentage of the literate public. Thus, when ʿAbd al-Karīm Ghallāb sets forth his goals in this regard:

> When I write, I am trying to speak to the public at large, all literate people, and not just the élite ...,[101]

his societal distinctions seem more a matter of political wishful thinking than of reality with regard to his potential audience. ʿAbd al-Ḥakīm Qāsim seems to hit the mark when he comments that:

> With regard to the question of literacy, I think the problem is that we're writing for the public at large (*shaʿb*), but that public does not read.[102]

When in the early 1930s H.A.R. Gibb wrote a series of articles on modern Arabic literature, he concluded one of them with the following;

> They (the Arab writers) know that what they are expressing is not the feeling of the people as a whole, but the view of a small minority who are striving, with increasing success and a strong assurance of ultimate victory, to convert and educate the people.[103]

After the series of post-World War revolutions in the Arab world and a succession of programmes to combat illiteracy, that "ultimate victory" has drawn closer. Qāsim's comment above may thus be as much concerned with persuading a new generation of Arab readers to undertake the task of reading *novels* (the demands of which were outlined in our citation of Q.D. Leavis above) rather than the question of literacy itself.

[100] *Fiction and the reading public*, London: Chatto and Windus, 1932, 205, 214-15, 224.
[101] *al-Ādāb* (Feb.-March 1980), 116.
[102] *al-Ādāb* (April-June 1980), 108.
[103] Reprinted in *Studies on the civilization of Islam*, 286.

Another practical matter which directly affects readership is that of book publication and distribution. We have already alluded to the direct connection of this subject to the internal politics of the various Arab countries, but it should also be noted that connections between the major book-publishing houses in the capitals of the Arab world are somewhat *ad hoc* and are among the first institutions to feel and reflect fluctuations in the political climate within the region. In happier times, international book fairs tend to assist in the process of circulating the works of authors in one country to the larger readership throughout the Arab world. Major novelists will generally benefit from better distribution and indeed from more critical attention in the literary periodicals, but problems of physical and political distance will often mean that the newer and lesser known novelists have a purely local readership, and—what may ultimately be a worse problem—their works may be only available in bookstores for a short while after publication (although it must be admitted that this latter problem is by no means restricted to the Arab world, as recent Internal Revenue decisions in the United States, whereby publishers may no longer discount the value of their stocks of current titles for tax purposes, make unfortunately clear).

Beyond these essentially practical and external questions relating to the issue of readership, what can be gleaned from the texts themselves? We refer here not to the complex web of relationships which exists between the novel text and the reader as analysed by Wolfgang Iser in his *The implied reader* (although the application of his ideas to the Arabic novel is just one of several agenda items for future research which lie beyond the goals of this introductory work), but rather to what Wellek and Warren (see below) refer to as "publics" while Q.D. Leavis talks in terms of "highbrow" and "lowbrow" works of fiction. Iḥsān ʿAbd al-Quddūs, for example, is believed to be the most popular novelist in the Arab world, by which is meant that his works have sold more copies than those of any other novelist. If this is indeed so, then the reasons are not hard to find. The female protagonist of *Anā ḥurra* ("I am free", n.d., 1950s) is typical of a number of works which have appealed to successive generations of adolescents and young adults faced with the task of reconciling traditional mores with the forces of change in the post-revolutionary Arab societies. This appeal has been intensified by ʿAbd al-Quddūs's choice of style and lexicon, both of which make few demands on the reader.

The causes of the fame of Najīb Maḥfūẓ are of a different order, in that he makes greater demands on his reader in theme, technique and language. One feature which he does share with ʿAbd al-Quddūs is an unwillingness to transcend the purely local environment. Maḥfūẓ has never visited the West (he is said to have paid a short, official visit to Yugoslavia); and this is reflected in his choice of setting for his novels. In spite of that fact, Maḥfūẓ was able in his novels written during the 1940s and 1950s to touch a sensitive nerve in several generations of educated Arabs, generations which had witnessed a common struggle against foreign occupation, the achievement of independence, and the search for new roles and values within the societies that emerged. And, just as his novels up to and including the *Trilogy* were vivid justifications for change, the novels of the 1960s reflected the concerns of that troubled decade and even identified some of the problems which June 1967 was to expose with embarrassing clarity. The declining readership for his works since that time may be seen perhaps as an indication of the inability or unwillingness of his generation of writers to adjust to new realities, and/or the desire of the broader readership in the Arab world to see their concerns reflected in new and original ways.

Many, if not most, Arabic novels are set in the local environment and thus introduce the reader to what is familiar in the spatial dimension at least, but this does not apply to all of them, as the analyses in the following chapter will show. The hero of al-Ṭayyib Ṣāliḥ's novel is completely at home in London and can recite English poetry, while the narrator in Ḥalīm Barakāt's *ʿAwdat al-ṭāʾir ilā al-baḥr* attributes to his hero Ramzī Ṣafadī a love of the music of Wagner and Rachmaninov and a knowledge of several American universities. But the novelist who seems to demand most of his reader is Jabrā Ibrāhīm Jabrā, whose works are full of references to painting, sculpture, music and literature. In the case of literature, this will mean poetry by both himself and others (from the classical period in the main); when European literature is cited, it is often incorporated into the text in the original language. Beyond this, there are discussions of classics of European literature with which the characters (and the reader) are presumed to be familiar and the mention of a variety of place-names. In the case of these novelists, the demands on the Arab reader reflect, of course, the experience and erudition of the writer, and in some instances that must certainly be the cause of exasperation on the reader's part. However, if alienation is, as we have suggested throughout this chapter, one of the principal themes of the modern Arabic novel, then the effort implicitly demanded of the reader in these cases may be seen as an attempt on the author's part to draw his reader into the alienated world which his novel strives to create. The wanderings and cosmopolitan outlook of the characters who people Jabrā's novels thus emerge as appropriate symbols of the exile in which the novelist and Palestinians share.

We have left till last the consideration of one particular kind of reader, namely the critic. Wellek and Warren term him "an important middle-man",[104] and yet the young Egyptian novelist Ṣanʿallāh Ibrāhīm lodges a complaint:

> The author looks to the critic for a clearer focus on—I won't say, solutions to—the problems he faces when writing. He expects a penetrating opinion, one which relies on a more comprehensive, analytical, comparative and experienced vision, something to which he can turn for guidance. However, except for rare instances, all Arab critics provide is something which is addressed solely to the reader.[105]

In writing this work, I have tried, as far as libraries in Western universities will permit, to survey as much critical opinion on the Arabic novel as possible, whether in book or journal form. With regard to reviews appearing in literary magazines, I would share Ibrāhīm's opinion *in general*. The majority do tend to take up most of their space in *describing* the plot of the novel and in discussing other "extrinsic" elements; the constructive and genuinely critical review tends to be the exception rather than the rule.[106] If the purview is expanded to include books, I have to repeat what I have previously stated elsewhere, namely that the majority of attention is devoted to the literary-historical approach rather than the strictly critical.[107] As the relative

[104] Rene Wellek and Austin Warren, *The theory of literature*, New York: Harcourt, Brace and World Inc., 1956, 100.

[105] *al-Ādāb* (Feb.-March 1980), 103.

[106] My own (albeit limited) experience suggests that *al-Ādāb* publishes reviews of a particularly high standard in this regard.

[107] See "Arabic literature", in *The study of the Middle East. Research in the humanities and social sciences*, New York: John Wiley, 1976, 428-36, 440-4, 508-9.

balances in the bibliography of this work will show, there is a plethora of works which discuss the history of the novel in such-and-such a country or the way in which the novel treats such-and-such a theme. The point to be made here is not that these works are inferior or useless (in the case of some national traditions, they are the only works available), but rather that such works tend not to be critical and thus do not respond to the needs expressed above by Ṣanʿallāh Ibrāhīm. However, before a hail of critical outrage descends, let me immediately state that the history of Western analysis of the novel shows precisely the same trends, at least until the last few decades. The relative sophistication which is currently evident in the analysis of narrative, be it the historical-theoretical approach of Lukacs, the investigation of narrative—its nature and tactics—by Wayne Booth and Scholes and Kellogg, or the variety of structural approaches demonstrated by a number of scholars writing originally in French, is not of great vintage. In the Arab world there already exists a small group of literary critics whose interests and writings transcend the barriers of geography or approach. Among those whose contributions appear to me particularly noteworthy are Shukrī ʿAyyād, Ilyās Khūrī, Khālida Saʿīd, Jurj Sālim, Maḥmūd al-Rabīʿī and Jabrā Ibrāhīm Jabrā. With regard to the application of some of the approaches just mentioned to the Arabic novel, mention should be made of recent articles by Ḍiyā' al-Sharqāwī and Ṭalāl Ḥarb, both of them structural in their analysis and concerned with novels discussed in our next chapter.[108]

Eight modern Arabic novels are now analysed; actually, since one analysis is concerned with a quartet, the number should probably be eleven. Each section does contain a description of the background and events of the work (in some instances, in so far as that is applicable), but in all cases an attempt is made to undertake a critical analysis of the work *per se* in the hope of adding to the corpus of works implicitly requested by Ibrāhīm in the quotation above.

[108] al-Sharqāwī, "al-Miʿmār al-fannī fī riwāyat al-Safīna", 7-57; and Ḥarb, "Fuṣḥat al-ikhtiyār: dirāsa bunyawiyya li-*Mā tabaqqā lakum*", *al-Ādāb* (July-Aug. 1980), 24-31.

CHAPTER IV

EIGHT ARABIC NOVELS

In the previous chapter, we attempted to show the various ways in which the tradition of the Arabic novel has expanded and developed following the Second World War, a process which has relied and built upon earlier experiments in the genre (the topic of our second chapter). Even within the confines of an introductory work such as this, it seems useful at this point to penetrate beyond the purely historical and descriptive aspects of our topic and to subject examples of the Arabic novel to an intrinsic analysis. In that way, those general traits and qualities which have been discussed in previous chapters within an investigation of the Arabic novel as a whole may be seen in the closer context of a single work by an individual author.

For this purpose, I have chosen eight novels for analysis. They are united by common features, but also separated by significant differences. On the basis of this collection of works, it is possible to suggest as an initial point of similarity that, as in other fictional traditions, the Arabic novel continues to be a genre which, in Lionel Trilling's words,

> most directly reveals to us the complexity, the difficulty, and the interest of life in society, and best instructs us in our human variety and contradiction.[1]

These novels have all been published within the last two decades, a period of vast and rapid change in the Arab world coupled with a considerable amount of political and social upheaval. The impact of the June 1967 War remains even today too fresh in the minds of many to receive a final assessment. With these facts in mind, it should come as no surprise that many of these novelists share with those of other world traditions an intense preoccupation with the concerns of intellectuals in society and particularly with their sense of alienation in the face of the individual and collective tensions of life in the modern world.

The differences in the works to be analysed reflect the complex nature of the novel genre itself. Of these, style is

[1] *The liberal imagination*, p. vii.

certainly one of the most immediately obvious, although unfortunately it is well-nigh impossible to reflect the subtleties of such differences through English translation and I have made no attempt to do so. In the sections which follow, therefore, the translated passages which are included should be regarded as illustrations of content alone. Another particular feature of these works is the variegated way in which the authors treat and manipulate time, preferring in many cases to operate in a narrative present, with its opportunities for interior monologue and stream of consciousness, and relying on flashbacks to fill in details from the past. A final element of difference is that of place, and here the variety in these novels is as broad as the Arab world itself: the settings in which characters are placed vary from boats at sea to the scorching heat of the desert or to the rainy cold of British universities, from the village with its entrenched traditional attitudes to the manifold complexities of the modern urban agglomeration.

These eight novels are not in any way an attempt on my part to assemble a list of "great Arabic novels". I hope that the previous chapter has given sufficient illustration of the variety and wealth of the tradition to show any such attempt to be folly, particularly in view of the lack of historical perspective involved. For we share with Salma al-Jayyusi the view that

> It will be for a future period to see more clearly than we can ever do now the genuine achievements of this period, [and to] differentiate the original experimentalists from the mere imitators ...[2]

She is in fact discussing the tradition of contemporary poetry, but the principle involved can be transferred to the novel with equal validity. It will nevertheless be observed that this has not prevented me from including in this list some extremely recent novels by authors whose names may not be familiar even to readers in the Arab world. Perhaps their early promise will fade away, or perhaps some mischance of history or (more likely) politics will condemn them to the same eventual obscurity as the Zelenkas and Hummels of eighteenth century European music. Let us hope not.

All of which is said in order to emphasise the fact that these eight novels are analysed here purely as illustrations of the contemporary tradition. They are works which I have read,

[2] *Trends and movements in modern Arabic poetry*, II, 605.

admired and found appropriate for intrinsic analysis. Other critics would almost certainly select a different list, but that may be seen as a reflection of the wealth which the tradition has to offer as well as being a matter of difference of opinion.

Bearing in mind the central role which Najīb Maḥfūẓ has been shown to play in bringing the Arabic novel to a higher artistic level, it is perhaps fitting that the first novel to be analysed should be by him.

1. *Tharthara fawq al-Nīl*
Najīb Maḥfūẓ

Those critics who have considered the group of novels which Najīb Maḥfūẓ published during the 1960s have generally tended to regard the first of the group, *al-Liṣṣ wa-al-kilāb* ("The thief and the dogs", 1961) as the best. Indeed, there is little doubt that this study of oppression and betrayal provides a most convincing fusion of symbol and reality in order to make some telling comments about socialist values. The fact that this work ends on such a negative note and that Maḥfūẓ's next novel, *al-Summān wa-al-kharīf* ("Quail and autumn", 1962), has such an optimistic conclusion may even suggest that there was some official concern about Maḥfūẓ's views as expressed in the first novel. In any case, I have always regarded *Tharthara fawq al-Nīl* ("Chatter on the Nile", 1966) as a work of equal distinction; in fact, in view of the extremely difficult task which Mahfūz sets himself in this later work, I find the results, if anything, even more impressive. In the first place, the spatial dimension in this novel is extremely restricted: the setting is an *ʿawwāma*, a houseboat on the Nile in Cairo. Within such an environment the action is, needless to say, confined, and one of the major features of the novel is an almost total lack of movement or change of scene. The narrative opens with a sarcastic description of the ministry office in which the novel's pivotal character, Anīs Zakī, works as a civil servant. He has finished a report and submitted it to his superior. He is summoned into the latter's office to explain how it is that the last pages of the report are completely blank; Anīs Zakī's pen has run dry in the process of writing the report and he has not even noticed.[3] Apart from this introduction to one of the situations in Anīs Zakī's life, the only

[3] *Tharthara fawq al-Nīl*, Cairo: Maktabat Miṣr, 1966, 7-8.

other occasion on which the scene shifts from the houseboat is when the characters of the novel pile into a car and go on a crazy ride down the Pyramids Road to Sakkāra, knock down and kill a peasant on the road, and do not stop to face the consequences.

The opening of the novel does more than depict the tedious environment of life in the civil service. In fact, that goal may be considered as ancillary to another literary task of some difficulty which Maḥfūẓ set himself in this work, namely of portraying Anīs Zakī in an almost permanently-drugged stupor, taciturn and inward-looking, hardly ever contributing to the "chatter" but responding to the comments of his superior in the ministry or his evening companions on the houseboat with streams of consciousness which resurrect episodes from past history and illustrate his own griefs and failures. The picture of Anīs Zakī's life and the activities on the houseboat which Maḥfūẓ gives is obviously important in that Anīs Zakī is, to quote one of the other characters, "in charge of our houseboat",[4] a phrase which has more than a merely surface import within the atmosphere which Maḥfūẓ creates in this novel. Further details and descriptions are provided at different stages of the work by other characters; Maḥfūẓ in this work is using a limited multi-narrator technique which he exploits to a fuller extent in his next work, *Mīrāmār*.[5] Less obviously than in *Mīrāmār* and other novels which Ḍiyā' al-Sharqāwī terms *riwāyāt ṣawtiyya*,[6] Maḥfūẓ in the present work uses the various narrative points of view to support or challenge the impressions—and that is all they are or are meant to be—which the reader has gained from the ramblings of Anīs Zakī's consciousness.

This then is not a novel of action; it is indeed concerned with "chatter on the Nile". The houseboat itself can, of course, be regarded as a means of detachment. It is moored to the land which in this case may be considered as the haven of a brutal reality, but the symbol of water allows for a lulling feeling of removal from such unpleasant facts of life which Anīs Zakī has to face in his office every day. It is from this environment that he escapes to his houseboat wafted by the cool evening breezes and

[4] *Ibid.*, 34.

[5] Cairo: Maktabat Miṣr, 1966; trans. Fatma Moussa-Mahmoud, see above, p. 59 n. 32.

[6] See *op. cit.*, 7 ff.

to the circle of companions who join him in the evening for encounters with drugs and sex. The symbolism implicit in this escape from land and reality is further underlined by the presence on the boat of ʿAmm ʿAbduh, the houseboat's general factotum, a huge man who, in addition to arranging all the necessary equipment for the evening's gathering and procuring girls for Anīs Zakī and the company when asked, also serves as Imām for a local group of Muslims. Throughout the work, ʿAmm ʿAbduh is a man of very few words; more often than not, his response is a cryptic "Ah". With this in mind, his forthright statement near the beginning of the narrative assumes a special importance:

I am the houseboat, because I am the ropes and lanterns. If for a single moment I did not do what I was supposed to do, the boat would sink and be carried away by the tide.[7]

ʿAmm ʿAbduh then is the guardian of the houseboat and the provider of all the needs and comforts for the group of individuals who come to share in the atmosphere of detached irreality which Anīs Zakī has created for himself.

The group who come to the houseboat are from a variety of professions: there is Muṣṭafā Rāshid, the lawyer; Khālid ʿAzūz the writer of short stories; Laylā Zaydān, a graduate of the American University in Cairo who has espoused feminist causes; Aḥmad Naṣr, a civil servant and book-keeper who is devoted to his wife and is described as "in sum a completely ordinary person";[8] ʿAlī al-Sayyid, an art critic and companion to Saniyya Kāmil, who, "at times of marital trouble comes back to her old friends, a woman of experience who learned all about womanhood while still a virgin, a wife and mother, who is a veritable treasure-house of experience for the young girls who come to our houseboat".[9] Much of the above description about these characters is given to the reader by Rajab al-Qāḍī, a celebrated film actor, who brings a new girl friend, Sanāʾ al-Rashīdī, to the group for the first time and introduces them to her one by one at the beginning of the fourth chapter. She is amazed at the blatant way in which the company indulges in illegalities, and this affords the characters—and, no doubt, the author—the opportunity to supply just one of a series of

[7] *Tharthara*, 15.
[8] *Ibid.*, 110.
[9] *Ibid.*, 34.

political comments which are scattered throughout the novel:

"Aren't you afraid of the police?" she asked.

"We're afraid of the police", ʿAlī al-Sayyid responded, "the army, the English, the Americans, the overt and the covert. It's reached the stage now that we're not afraid of anything."

"But the door is wide open!"

"ʿAmm ʿAbduh is outside. He can keep out any intruders."

"Don't worry, gorgeous," Rajab said with a smile, "the government's so busy building things, it hasn't got time to bother us."

"Why don't you try this type of fortitude?" asked Muṣṭafā Rāshid, offering her the hashish pipe.[10]

The cynicism of the group, the reliance on ʿAmm ʿAbduh, and the desire to run away from reality and to persuade others to do so, all these features are evident in this short extract. Into this situation comes the figure of Sammāra Bahjat. We first hear of her at the beginning of the fifth chapter[11] when ʿAlī al-Sayyid announces that his journalistic colleague wants to visit them, since her curiosity has been aroused both by his conversations to her about the group and also by the publications in a variety of media of the artists who frequent the group. It is this same Sammāra Bahjat who provides another level of insight into the characters on the houseboat when, in the tenth chapter,[12] Anīs Zakī reads from her diary the outline of a play which she has written, one in which all the personae are taken from the group on the houseboat. She has provided a cameo sketch of each of the "characters" in her play which reflects her own opinion of the person concerned. She has, in fact, told them earlier of her extreme interest in the theatre as something which "has focus and where every word has to have its own particular meaning".[13] She ignores Muṣṭafā Rāshid's retort to this comment, to the effect that the theatre is thus totally opposite to what goes on on the houseboat, and instead asks the stupefied Anīs Zakī why he is not saying anything. This sends Anīs off on one of his journeys into history and his own consciousness, and yet typically he makes no response.

As Sammāra begins to attend the group regularly, they begin to worry about the fact that she is too serious; she poses a threat

[10] *Ibid.*, 36-37.
[11] *Ibid.*, 46.
[12] *Ibid.*, 107 ff.
[13] *Ibid.*, 61.

to their escapism. As Muṣṭafā Rāshid asks, "Do you think she's planning to make us all serious some time?",[14] to which Khālid ʿAzūz responds that Rajab al-Qāḍī seems to have his own plans with regard to Sammāra. As if to confirm this possibility, Sanāʾ no longer appears with Rajab at the group's gatherings.

After Anīs Zakī has read Sammāra's diary which, unknown to the group, contains her impressions based on these conversations, an amusing chapter follows in which he argues with the group about their priorities in life, quoting throughout from Sammāra's diary. Even though he does not reveal the source of his comments and the group seems only moderately disturbed by his unusual loquaciousness, Sammāra herself feels most uneasy and eventually succeeds in getting the diary back after refusing to sleep with him.[15] The fact that Anīs Zakī serves as a mouthpiece for the views of Sammāra about the group may perhaps be seen as a premonition of what is to come. When the grossly-overcrowded car in which they are speeding along the Pyramid Road kills the peasant, Sammāra insists that they stop, true to her role within the group and confirming their fears about her. Anīs Zakī is unable to sleep and only succeeds in doing so at his desk the next day, whereupon he is arrested after assaulting the Director General who has reprimanded him for his conduct.[16] When the group meets that night, the atmosphere is tense. Sammāra insists that they go to the police, whereas everyone else is afraid of being exposed. Their efforts to point out to her that her own reputation will also be soiled are of no avail. Rajab al-Qāḍī, the driver of the car and would-be lover of Sammāra, becomes increasingly furious at Anīs Zakī's comments, and a terrible fight ensues, during which the figure of ʿAmm ʿAbduh appears, only to be sent away again by Aḥmad Naṣr.[17] However, the group is not ready for the consequence of this fracas; for, when Anīs Zakī recovers, it is to tell his colleagues that murder is one thing which cannot be taken lightly, and he makes it clear that he is referring to the death of the peasant on the road.[18] He says unequivocally that he is fully cognisant of what he is saying and that he will go to the police

[14] *Ibid.*, 80.
[15] *Ibid.*, 133.
[16] *Ibid.*, 173.
[17] *Ibid.*, 186.
[18] *Ibid.*, 187.

himself. Rajab tries to attack again, but the group take him away. ʿAmm ʿAbduh now reappears with a cup of coffee which, he hints, will make him feel better. Anīs Zakī is now left with Sammāra, and she only has time for a short conversation about the implications of their position before the laced coffee sends Anīs Zakī off into a final reverie concerning the tragedy of man's evolution "from the paradise of apes in trees to the ground in the forest".[19]

From this brief, yet somewhat complex description, it will, I hope, be clear that we are dealing with one of Maḥfūẓ's richest essays in the use of symbolism. We have already made several suggestions on this topic, but the store is by no means exhausted. It should, for example, be pointed out that all the members of the group which meets on the houseboat belong to the intellectual class and more specifically to those in the sphere of culture.[20] That Maḥfūẓ should have addressed himself to the issues evoked by the problems, life style and expectations of this group during the period of the early 1960s is in itself of extreme significance. For, as many people have since shown and as Maḥfūẓ himself has recorded in more recent fictional works such as *al-Marāyā* ("Mirrors", 1972)[21] and *al-Karnak* (the name of a café, 1974),[22] these years may have witnessed some of the most oppressive political constraints on the artist during the entire revolutionary period. But, to remain on a more literary plane, one may observe at the very least that the characters who join Anīs Zakī in the evening are escaping into a world where they can forget or ignore aspects of their own reality. No doubt the socio-political conditions to which we have just alluded play a part in this desire to escape, but each character has his or her own reasons for doing so, some of them rooted in the past, others impinging from the present. In the case of Anīs Zakī, these include his failure to complete a degree programme at a number of colleges, his loss of both his wife and daughter, and the continuing tedium and frustration of his job. Perhaps the most remarkable example of all is Aḥmad Naṣr, who is

[19] *Ibid.*, 199.

[20] Compare Jabrā's *The Ship* (discussed below), in which a boat is again used as a refuge in which a group of Arab intellectuals discuss their problems.

[21] *al-Marāyā* (Mirrors), Cairo: Maktabat Miṣr, 1972; transl. Allen, see above p. 60 n. 33.

[22] See Allen, "Some recent works of Najīb Mahfūz", 105 ff.

described by both Rajab al-Qāḍī and Sammāra Bahjat as a successful civil servant and loyal husband. And yet he too feels the need to resort to this group of individuals; to Sammāra Bahjat, the very security of his business and family life may leave him deep down with a sense of futility in that nothing in life seems to change pace.[23] The various roads to escape which the group follows by coming to the houseboat are first challenged and then dashed by the inquiries and convictions of Sammāra Bahjat. Rajab al-Qāḍī, the great lover, is unable to win her love or to persuade her not to go to the police. When she seems on the point of relenting, it is Anīs Zakī, the taciturn, sombre master of ceremonies, who finally, in his own words, "wanted to try saying the things which need to be said!"[24]

A final word needs to be said about Maḥfūẓ's use of language in this novel. It has been my impression from reading Maḥfūẓ's novels for a number of years that his total lexicon is not particularly large and that his style lacks the more poetic qualities of some other Arab novelists, including Jabrā Ibrāhīm Jabrā and ʿAbd al-Raḥmān Munīf, whose works are discussed below. Maḥfūẓ's style tends to reflect the skills of a careful craftsman who has spent much of his life as a civil servant and who writes very much on a regular, almost routine, basis. In this aspect, I would contrast his style with that of his younger fellow-countryman, Yūsuf Idrīs, whose style seems more spontaneous and impulsive, on occasion almost to the point of irregularity.[25] I should make it clear that my comments here are intended to be more a description of differences in style than a criticism of the writer whose name personifies the Arabic novel's achievement of genuine maturity. What I am suggesting with reference to *Tharthara fawq al-Nīl* is that Maḥfūẓ used his lexicon with consummate artistry to fuse together in a single, cryptic atmosphere the various elements of the overt and covert, the conscious and unconscious, the present and the past, all of which provide us with such a rich store of symbols to depict the role and fate of the Egyptian cultural intelligentsia during the 1960s.

[23] *Tharthara*, 110.
[24] *Ibid.*, 195.
[25] For a similar opinion, see Sulaymān Fayyāḍ in *Kutub ʿarabiyya* no. 1 (Jan. 1977), 2.

2. *Mā tabaqqā lakum*
Ghassān Kanafānī

No modern Arab novelist has been able to project the tragedy of the Palestinian people in fiction with greater impact than Ghassān Kanafānī. That is hardly surprising in view of the fact that he devoted his life to the illustration in both fact and fiction of the circumstances of the Palestinians and to an investigation of the complexities of Arab attitudes to them. Into a short life of thirty-six years he managed to fit a career as an increasingly experimental writer of fiction and that of spokesman for the Popular Front for the Liberation of Palestine.

Of all his works of fiction, *Rijāl fī al-shams* ("Men in the sun", 1963) is undoubtedly the most famous, and its message concerning the inability of Palestinians to find a place or role for themselves in the glare of harsh reality and their exploitation by Arabs of other nationalities is conveyed with tremendous clarity and force. In fact, in spite of the excellent use of imagery in this work and the careful way in which the plot is constructed, the impact of the symbolism is, in my opinion, too clear and forceful. It is for that reason that I have chosen another novel which broaches the same theme, the plight of the Palestinians, in a more subtle fashion, namely *Mā tabaqqā lakum* ("What remains for you", 1966). Furthermore, from the technical point of view, the latter novel has a number of interesting experimental features which show the ways in which the writer was developing his artistry.

In a "clarification" at the beginning of this novel, Kanafānī makes it clear that he has been particularly aware of matters of technique in writing this work:

> The five heroes of this novel, Ḥāmid, Maryam, Zakariyyā, Time and the Desert, do not move in parallel lines or opposite directions. That much will be obvious from the very start. Rather they intersect in a way which is so compact that they all seem to make just two separate threads. This compactness also includes time and place to such an extent that there will be no specific dividing line between places which are far apart or between different time frames, and sometimes even between time and place at one and the same time.[26]

[26] *al-Āthar al-kāmila. I, al-Riwāyāt*, Beirut: Dār al-Ṭalīʿa, 1972, 159. I should add parenthetically that Ṭalāl Ḥarb's structural analysis of this novel (*al-Ādāb*, July-Aug. 1980) came to my attention too late to be incorporated into this analysis of the novel.

This statement raises a number of interesting points regarding the novelist's technique, but one of the most striking is the almost nonchalant juxtaposition of the elements of time and place—in this case the desert—with the three main characters of the work as being "heroes" (*abṭāl*), a usage which recalls the partial ancestry of the novel genre in the older epic tradition, as was noted in our introductory chapter. In this novel, time does indeed play a pivotal role. The events take place over an interval of some eighteen hours, most of them being at night; the background is filled in here, as in so many of these novels which we are surveying, through the generous use of flashback. But time is also a more obtrusive protagonist in this work, and its role is symbolised in two instruments which tell time: a wall clock whose ticking punctuates the life of those who live in the Palestinian home which is the major focus of the action, and a watch which the hero, Ḥāmid, discards as useless on his journey through the desert.

It will be recalled that in *Rijāl fī al-shams*, the desert had represented not only a barrier to be traversed but also a place of scorching heat, a heat which led to the deaths of the Palestinians inside the water-tank. In *Mā tabaqqā lakum*, the desert is once again a barrier, in fact it is now a barrier which has to be crossed in a short time in order to avoid Israeli border patrols, but for that same reason it has to be crossed at night. Our hero is therefore not concerned with the problems of heat (except for a short time on the second day). His major concern is with cold and the loneliness of the dark desert wastes when every light and every sound seems magnified a thousand times, even the ticking of his watch. And, just as *Rijāl fī al-shams* opens with Abū Qays lying on the ground feeling the heartbeat of the earth beneath him,[27] in *Mā tabaqqā lakum* Ḥāmid throws himself to the ground

> and felt it shuddering beneath him like a virgin as a beam of light silently and softly swept across the folds of sand. Just at that moment he rivetted himself to the ground and felt it soft and warm.[28]

In another telling juxtaposition, the beats of the earth beneath Ḥāmid's prostrate body find themselves associated with the foetus inside his sister's womb. In this way, the decisions of brother and sister which form the focus of this novel are, as the

[27] *al-Āthār al-kāmila*. I, 37.
[28] *Ibid*., 169; see also 161.

author noted above, brought together in spite of a distance in time and space.

But what of the characters themselves? Ḥāmid and Maryam are brother and sister who, in the rush to leave in 1948, were separated from their mother; she now lives in Jordan while they are quartered in a refugee camp in the Gaza Strip. The two children have been cared for by an aunt, and it is significant that her death is marked, as are so many episodes in this novel, by the chiming of the wall clock.[29] Ḥāmid is almost twenty years younger than his sister, Maryam, but in spite of this his aunt has repeatedly urged him, as the man of the family, to get his sister married. Maryam is thirty-five years old now and has managed all that time to maintain her chastity. But, as if to confirm her aunt's worst fears, her one "slip" (as she explains it to her brother) is a costly one for the family as a whole.[30] She becomes pregnant and persuades the father of the child to marry her. Normally this might be considered a happy solution to the problem, but not in this case. For the father is none other than Zakariyyā who is already married and has five children.[31] In the context of the fate of Palestine and its people, even that is not the major problem. In a telling flashback, Ḥāmid records how a few years earlier a young man named Sālim had been involved in underground activities against the Israeli armed forces. All the boys of the camp had been lined up, and Sālim had been told to step forward. No one had moved, but at the first sign of threat from the soldiers, Zakariyyā had given way; Sālim duly stepped forward, and was taken away and shot in their hearing.[32]

Thus, as far as Ḥāmid and most of his contemporaries are concerned, Maryam's enforced and all-too-obliging husband is a symbol of all that is despicable and loathsome, a personification of betrayal of the Palestinian cause from within. To make matters worse, Zakariyyā begins to treat the house of his new wife as his own, using it as a kind of way station between the place where he works and his other home where Fatḥiyya, his wife, and their children live. All this proves too much for Ḥāmid to bear. He decides to leave for Jordan in search of his

[29] *Ibid.*, 174.
[30] *Ibid.*, 180.
[31] *Ibid.*, 188.
[32] *Ibid.*, 76, 200, 212-15.

mother, in spite of all the risks involved. The stage is thus set for the action of the novel itself: Maryam remains in what is left of the family home in Gaza trying to resolve the conflict between the fact that she is married to Zakariyyā and carrying his child, while her own brother is attempting to cross at night a desert full of natural and human obstacles and dangers; Ḥāmid meanwhile has abandoned his intolerable reality in Gaza and gone in seach of his mother, a symbol of security and family honour.

It is within this framework so rich in potential that the technique of Ghassān Kanafānī, outlined in the above quotation, emerges as such an interesting and, in my opinion, successful portrayal of the complexities of the situation, even though, as the author himself admits, the need to distinguish speakers and time frames through the use of differing type-faces tends to complicate the process somewhat. Throughout the long night of Ḥāmid's traversal of the frontier, Maryam is unable to sleep. She feels inside herself the pulsating beat of his footsteps which are mingled with the ticking of the clock and the movements of the baby which she is carrying. Initially, Ḥāmid too is linked to her by the ticking of his watch, but when he discards it, the sound is replaced by the pulsating of the earth beneath him. Maryam's wakefulness disturbs Zakariyyā, and he tries to persuade his new bride to forget about her immature and impetuous brother who has embarked on such a foolhardy expedition. She tells him that the foetus of their child is keeping her awake, and to the sound of the chiming clock—once again—he tells her what a scandal will be created by the birth of the child so soon after their marriage and suggests that she have an abortion.[33] Maryam now comes to realize what a fateful decision she has made in marrying Zakariyyā and what an opportunist and coward he really is. The horror of this realisation is accompanied by the beat of Ḥāmid's footsteps moving ever further away across the desert.[34]

As the novel draws to its climax, brother and sister are both face to face with the enemy, without or within. Ḥāmid surprises an Israeli border guard and subdues him. The realisation gradually dawns on him that, if he is to reach Jordan, he will have to kill his captive. Zakariyyā meanwhile threatens his

[33] *Ibid.*, 222-3.
[34] *Ibid.*, 225.

sister with divorce if she does not have an abortion. When he starts to beat her, she grabs a knife. In both the desert and house scenarios, the eerie sound of howling dogs is to be heard. Maryam stabs her husband to death in a gesture which is made to suffice for both situations. The enemy which has brought this family so low on both the general and particular planes has been eradicated.

The above analysis of the plot of this novel has shown clearly Kanafānī's rich and skilful use of symbols, and they are accompanied and embellished by an attractive imagery. We have already mentioned the description of the earth as a breathing, pulsating creature. Equally forceful is the way in which Kanafānī portrays that crucial moment when Ḥāmid realizes that his sister is pregnant:

She sat down and wrapped her arms round her waist. My eye fell on them and suddenly I realised. I was overcome by panic and beads of perspiration started falling from my forehead into my eyes. I felt as though a cry was emerging from beneath her hands wrapped round her waist, a wounded cry which seemed to be coming from between her thighs where she had put her hands as though to hide something. And then suddenly she began to cry.[35]

Imagery and symbols such as these are used with great effect in most, if not all, of Kanafānī's fictional writings. What is different and consciously experimental about *Mā tabaqqā lakum* is the narrative technique. The two protagonists, Ḥāmid and Maryam, also serve as the principal narrators; for this purpose both first and third person, narrative past and present, are used. Changes in mode or person are marked by a change of type face; in the following examples, the heavy type face will be represented by italics:

He was relying entirely on his senses, a single impulse enveloped in a certain amount of fear. But even that had a sense of excitement about it. A whole grab-bag of feelings filling the clenched fists of a plucky adventurer as they pound on some unknown portal. I was quivering with heat and excited at one and the same time when I saw him at the door. Ḥāmid had left just five minutes before, and now here was Zakariyyā standing at the door full of self-confidence and asking whether he was still here.[36]

In this instance, Arabic can convey what English cannot: the adjectives which qualify the "I" following the italicised section

[35] *Ibid.*, 175.
[36] *Ibid.*, 178.

are in the feminine and thus make it clear to the reader that the "he" of the italicised section is Ḥāmid in the course of his desert journey, while the "I" of the second segment is Maryam recounting the fateful occasion when Zakariyyā seduced her. In addition to the fact that these two episodes are joined to each other directly, it is worth noticing that, in spite of the vastly different situations involved, brother and sister are shown here to share the same combination of fear and excitement.

Occasionally this switching of time and place can be very rapid:

Here I am once again faced with a fresh moment in time which I don't know how to handle. At first I started to smile and then suddenly I burst into fits of laughter. Zakariyyā rolled over on to his side and looked at me, then rolled back again and went to sleep as though he too were deeply involved in some insane dream. *You may know Hebrew and nothing else but that doesn't matter. Just listen. Isn't it really infuriating that we should meet face to face in this wilderness in the way we did, and yet be unable to talk to each other? He continued to stare at me, enigmatic, hesitant, somewhat doubtful, but certainly scared.* For my part I had gone beyond being scared; the feeling I had now was strange and inexplicable.[37]

Here in the space of a few lines, the situation moves twice from Ḥāmid confronted with the problem of the Israeli guard to Maryam lying in bed with her husband thinking about her brother. Also noteworthy in this passage is the way in which the person is changed in each of the four segments.

In one final example of this technique there is a switch of persons while a single narrator, in this case Ḥāmid, is recounting his situation:

He got up and stood on his feet. He began to look around him, probing with his eyes into the darkness for a sign of anything. Then he came back. He began to search the Israeli's pocket. My fingers felt his soft wallet, so I took it out and began to look through it. It was hard to know what value any of the papers had because it was so dark, and so I put them all into my shirt pocket.[38]

The effect here is almost cinematic, as the change from third to first person almost palpably brings the narrative lens closer to the scene of the action. The tremendous closeness of Ḥāmid to his anonymous Israeli foe is made even more striking by the fact that, immediately after the extract just quoted, Ḥāmid records

[37] *Ibid.*, 208.
[38] *Ibid.*, 212.

the inevitable realisation by the Israeli soldier that the only possible end to this episode is his—the Israeli's—death.

Kanafānī's life was one of commitment to the cause of the Palestinian people. However, his fictional writings do not show that concern with magnified realism which marks or even disfigures the works of less artistic commentators on the Palestinian cause. His literary career is marked by a constant concern with form, style and imagery. While *Mā tabaqqā lakum* has not emerged as his most popular work of fiction, it remains a subtle and innovative treatment of this most popular of topics for modern Arab authors, and a remarkable contribution to the development of narrative modes in Arabic fiction.

3. *'Awdat al-ṭā'ir ilā al-baḥr*
Ḥalīm Barakāt

The Flying Dutchman has now returned to the sea. But he still feels an intense longing for the land. He cannot remain in exile and without roots for ever.[39]

In this novel, *The return of the Flying Dutchman to the sea* (translated by Trevor Le Gassick as *Days of dust*),[40] the Syrian-born writer Ḥalīm Barakāt gives us one of the most cogent and realistic pictures of the events of 1967 and of the way in which they reflect on Arab society in general. Since Barakāt is himself a sociologist by training, this latter aspect is one of the most prominent features of the work, affecting the portrayal of character and narrative point of view in no small way. Indeed, the character through whose consciousness the story of the Flying Dutchman—the sailor condemned to roam the seas until he is redeemed by the discovery of true love—is filtered is Ramzī Ṣafadī, a professor at the American University in Beirut. And it is Barakāt himself who reminds us that "Ramzī" is the Arabic for "my symbol" or even "the symbol of me".[41] Through Ramzī Ṣafadī, the Palestinian, Western-trained professor living in exile in Beirut, the Flying Dutchman becomes a symbol of the continuing agony of the Palestinian people; like the sailor for ever roaming the seas, they too continue to meet

[39] *'Awdat al-ṭā'ir ilā al-baḥr* Beirut: Dār al-Nahār, 1969, 161.

[40] Wilmette, Illinois: Medina Press International, 1974.

[41] *Visions of social reality in the contemporary Arab novel*, 37. Khālida Sa'īd points out that Barakāt himself went on a mission to Jordan after the June War. See *Mawāqif* 5 (July-Aug. 1969), 176, n. 1.

devastating failure in their attempts to regain their land. To Ramzī, as to most other Palestinians, this exile goes back to the fighting in 1948, an event captured in an earlier novel by Barakāt, which he called *Sittat ayyām* ("Six days", 1961, discussed in the previous chapter) in an almost ill-starred prediction of the course of events in the 1967 conflict and therefore of the present work itself.

As Ramzī has this final thought about the Flying Dutchman, he is standing on a hill overlooking Amman, where he has come with a group of his colleagues and students to investigate the real extent of the disaster. In order to give his impressions a particular force, Barakāt again resorts to an extraneous source, in this case the Bible and more specifically the Book of Genesis. The final chapter of the novel, "Ayyām ʿadīda min al-ghubār" ("Many days of dust"), begins:

> On the seventh day, he did not rest. Sadly his seventh day is not a single day. He has no idea how long into the future it will last. ... Everything that the Arab created in the first six days was dust ... Darkness returns to cover the earth ... the earth becomes desolate and void, and darkness is on the face of the deep. It is the beginning of creation. But the spirit of God does not move on the face of the waters. The Arab says, "Let there be light", but there is none. He cannot distinguish light from darkness. ... The Arab saw everything that he had made, and behold, it was very bad. For that reason he did not rest on the seventh day. He is trying to erase the traces of the dominion of fishes, birds and other creatures from his body. The future is all that he has.[42]

With these evocative, yet damning thoughts, Ramzī brings the reader back to the beginning of the work; for the first chapter, "al-ʿAtaba" ("The threshold") is set in the same location and uses the beginning of Genesis with the same telling effect. These two chapters are indeed a frame within which the narrative of the fateful "six days" of June 1967 is set. Characters, symbols and images from the central chapters find their way into these two outlying chapters, but the moral for the Arabs of the future is laid out with brutal clarity in these two chapters. The central narrative, with its almost cinematic realism, has its own impact, needless to say; but the first and last chapters, with their use of the narrative present (even in the

[42] *ʿAwda*, 147.

Genesis parody), show us that, after such a total defeat, the future is all the Arab has.

Apart from these first and last chapters when Ramzī is in Amman, the rest of the novel finds him and his colleagues in Beirut. The choice of this location serves the author's purpose admirably. Perhaps most forcefully, it permits the portrayal of an entire people being led by their leaders to believe that they are at last on the way to total victory over the Israelis; news broadcasts from throughout the Arab world talk about crushing defeats of the enemy, enemy planes being downed and tremendous heroism by the Arab fighting forces. The enthusiasm and sense of resurgence among some of Ramzī's students is almost palpable. And then comes the shattering news of total defeat, a defeat almost from the very start. Shock is followed by bitterness, by attacks on the American and British Embassies in Beirut (on the basis of yet another news report), by Nasser's speech of resignation and the swirling violence of a huge demonstration in support of the Egyptian leader. The steady rise and abrupt crash of this corporate emotion during these six days is callously manipulated by the news media, a point which Barakāt underlines with unconcealed anger and which another Syrian writer of fiction, Zakariyyā Tāmir, carries even further in his short story *al-Aʿdāʾ* ("The enemies"), in which the Arabic language is given an award for heroism for downing so many planes and immobilising so many tanks in the war.[43] Ramzī's description of or participation in the events in Beirut mentioned above provides us with a most effective picture of the way in which the impact of this defeat was felt by the Arabs. It was not merely a total defeat, but one which was inflicted on a people who were being led by their governments to believe right up to the very last moment that they were scoring a resounding victory. Worst of all, the instantaneous loss of the air battle and complete superiority of the Israeli air force made the June war for the Arabs a defeat without heroism.

It is precisely Beirut's distance from the actual fighting which permits the impact of these vicious lessons to strike home. Many of them are discussed by Ramzī with Pamela, a beautiful

[43] Zakariyyā Tāmir, "al-Aʿdāʾ" in *al-Numūr fī al-yawm al-ʿāshir*, Beirut: Dār al-Ādāb, 1978, 5 ff.; trans. Roger Allen "The enemies", *Nimrod* XXIV/2 (Spring-Summer 1981), 61-70.

American artist separated from her husband. Their torrid relationship serves to divert Ramzī's attentions temporarily from what is going on in the fighting; there are some telling juxtapositions of the two of them making love and the scene as planes rain destruction on the West Bank.[44] Pamela herself, foot-loose, unsure of her relationships with both her husband and Ramzī, and not a little selfish, may serve, as Ilyās Khūrī suggests, as a symbol of "the approaching breakdown of Western capitalism"[45] within Barakāt's revolutionary intentions for Arab society.[46] But it would appear that her most valuable function within Barakāt's larger purpose in writing this novel is to serve as a sounding board for Ramzī's views on Arab society, its traditions and values. The availability of Pamela, the beautiful American tourist with *Wanderlust*, to discuss issues which burn in the mind of "my symbol" (Ramzī) is most convenient to the didactic purpose of the novel.

Beirut in this novel is far from the fighting, and yet to Ramzī, the exiled Palestinian, it is tantalisingly near; so much so that it arouses his guilt feelings for not being there, feelings which become particularly evident when he is making love to Pamela. Part of his mind is always in Palestine, and never more so than during these climactic days. Ramzī joins all the other Palestinians in a single experience, and Barakāt's narrative technique is a major element in the attempt to portray such a feeling of unity.

In the six central chapters, each one devoted to a day in the conflict, Beirut (with Ramzī and Pamela) is just one of a number of locations. Prominent attention is also given to Ṭāhā Kanʿān in Jericho, Khālid ʿAbd al-Ḥalīm in Sabastiya, and ʿAzmī ʿAbd al-Qādir in Jerusalem. We are also given flashes of information about other figures in numerous villages and towns on the West Bank. Even here, the activities and discussions of Ramzī and Pamela remain the central thread in the narrative, but at the same time there is a continuous sweeping of Barakāt's verbal camera from one battleground to another. These brief and realistic depictions of the futile attempts at organising resistance on the West Bank, followed rapidly by the shattering realisation of impotence and headlong flight towards the River

44 *ʿAwda*, 90-1, 108.
45 *Tajribat al-baḥth ʿan ufq*, Beirut: P.L.O. Research Center, 1974, 67.
46 Barakat, *Visions*, 36.

Jordan, are rarely more than one or two pages in length; the speed at which the reader is transferred from one to the next helps to emphasise within the narrative the alarming rapidity with which the events themselves happened. At times, this pace reaches prestissimo:

Ramzī scrutinises this country, eager to find out if it's full of grain. 'Azmi 'Abd al-Qādir encircled in Jerusalem. Ṭāhā weeping in hospital. Khālid looking askance at his flute. Māhir searching. Abū Dahhām longing to have a ruined house of his own in Qalqīliya. Ramzī checking the ears in search of grain.[47]

Khālid's family is a tissue of fractious relationships, and the decision to abandon their home, though hard, is not as difficult as it is for Ṭāhā who tries to organise the local resistance and is still trying to reach the authorities by telephone when events overtake him and he too decides to leave. Khālid's family reaches Amman safely,[48] whereas Ṭāhā's family pays heavily for the delay in leaving. In the narrative of the third day, aptly entitled *al-Mawt ḥaql* ("Death is a field"), they are bombed with napalm just after crossing the River Jordan. In a passage of gruesome realism Barakāt describes the futile attempts of the father to put out the flames which are enveloping his children.[49] While Ṭāhā continues to Amman with his two remaining children (one of whom will also die), 'Azmī stays resolutely behind in Jerusalem. He has been waiting for the opportunity to fight again ever since 1948, and, even when his house and entire family are destroyed in the fighting and it becomes abundantly clear that this round is going to end in complete defeat for the Arabs, he still refuses to leave. The Sister at a local hospital helps him to load his family on to a cart, but at this moment Israeli soldiers arrive and search the hospital. 'Azmī escapes through a window and is last heard of "encircled in Jerusalem".[50]

This fusion of the spatial dimension into a single experience through time serves the author's purpose well; we do indeed come to feel that those who find themselves faced with the reality of the military might of Israel and the weaknesses of the

[47] *'Awda*, 143. For a similar narrative technique, albeit less hectic, see 35-6, 41-4, 64-7.
[48] *Ibid.*, 83.
[49] *Ibid.*, 87.
[50] *Ibid.*, 143.

Arabs—whether from close-up or from a distance—are united in their attempts to cope with the situation and in their failure to find satisfactory explanations or conclusions. However, this technique also involves sacrifices in certain aspects of novelistic technique, and no more so than in characterisation. The rapidity with which the scene is transferred from one battle-scene to another does not afford much opportunity, needless to say, for characterisation of the various figures in different towns and villages in which the fighting occurs. However, it is perhaps more surprising that we learn relatively little about Ramzī and Pamela too. Part of the reason for this may refer to an earlier comment about Ramzī as meaning "my symbol". If we also suggest that Pamela is a symbol of a decadent West, then the relationship between the two may be seen as essentially a game of symbols rather than a profound investigation into two individual characters. This impression is emphasised by the fact that Barakāt uses—one might almost say, manipulates—these characters in order to indulge in the kind of social commentary which used to characterise novels of a much earlier period (although, admittedly here, without the heavy overlay of moral judgement). Certain issues which are discussed by these two characters may indeed be fused into the general interchange of ideas as emotions of two people of different cultures thrown together during an international crisis: American attitudes towards the Arabs and the somewhat ivory-tower attitude of students in universities in the Arab world are two examples.[51] But in other cases, the inclusion of certain issues into the conversation between Ramzī and Pamela or into the thoughts of Ramzī himself seems contrived in the extreme: consider, for example, the discussions of Arab "anti-Semitism" and the fate of the Palestinian refugees on the one hand, and Ramzī's ideas and hopes about the future of the Arab world on the other.[52] All these issues are entirely germane to the subject of the Palestinian tragedy and the 1967 defeat as they reflect on the Arab world in general. However, the point to be made here is that, in his desire to use certain techniques of realism in portraying both the background and events of this traumatic episode in the history of the Arab world, Barakāt has de-emphasised characterisation

[51] *Ibid.*, 75-6 and 45 respectively.
[52] *Ibid.*, 96 and 123; 23 and 157.

and over-emphasised the documentary aspect to a degree which diminishes the artistic merit of the work as a whole.[53]

There are times in this work when the reader almost gets the impression that Barakāt is addressing his ideas and comments to a Western audience. Within this chapter, we note in connection with other modern Arabic novels (such as Jabrā's *al-Safīna*) that they presuppose a relatively profound knowledge of Western culture. Barakāt's work includes references to Wagner, Toynbee, T.S. Eliot, Rachmaninov and Camus.[54] The impact of these and analogous references in works by other Arab novelists has been considered in our previous chapter, but within the context of this particular novel we should point out that references to particular universities in the United States and remarks on the anti-Arab feelings of American periodicals seem to be addressed more to an American audience than an Arab one. Typically, Barakāt expresses the dilemma of himself and others on this matter in the words of one of his characters:

> What concerns me is that we're a people which has lost its sense of identity and manhood. Each one of us suffers from a split personality, particularly in Lebanon. We're Arabs, and yet our education may be French, Anglo-Saxon or Eastern-mystic. What an odd mixture! We need to go back to our roots. We're all schizophrenic.[55]

If this novel has faults in particular aspects of construction, the overall impression is undeniably powerful; the impact of the synchronic treatment of events during this fatal six-day period is considerable. Barakāt's work stands out as one of the most effective commentaries on the 1967 débâcle and its implications, and, one may say, almost *ipso facto*, it will remain a monument of Arabic fiction written during this century.

4. *Ayyām al-insān al-sab'a*
'Abd al-Ḥakīm Qāsim

We noted above the almost cruel irony that Ḥalīm Barakāt gave to his first novel about the 1948 conflict in Palestine the title *Sittat ayyām* ("Six days"). The bitter lessons of the Six-Day

[53] Compare the verdict of George Sālim about this novel: "In my view, the value of this work lies in its reliance on a new artistic style. But for this style, this new technique, it would lose all its value". See *al-Mughāmara al-riwā'iyya*, 179.

[54] *Ibid.*, 28, 32, 68, 120, 75.

[55] *Ibid.*, 55.

War of June 1967 imposed upon his second novel, *'Awdat al-ṭā'ir ilā al-baḥr*, an identical chronological framework, although, as we noted above, Barakāt succeeds very well in manipulating the dictates of time to his own literary ends. Both these works are, needless to say, directly concerned with crucial political events which have had a profound effect on the entire Middle East.

The "seven days" of 'Abd al-Ḥakīm Qāsim's novel, *Ayyām al-insān al-sab'a* ("The seven days of man", 1969), could scarcely provide a greater contrast.[56] International politics barely enter the narrative at all, and then only as an intruding entity brought in by the radio and its news broadcasts. The setting here is the Egyptian countryside, and that environment provides a link with a whole series of earlier works, although, in my opinion, the present novel is the best.[57]

The "seven days" of the title are seven stages followed by a group of dervishes in the Delta of Egypt in the process of preparing for the annual pilgrimage to the shrine of al-Sayyid al-Badawī, one of the great "saints" of popular Islam in Egypt, which is situated in the Delta city of Ṭanṭā. The series of events is narrated for us through the eyes of 'Abd al-'Azīz, the son of al-Ḥājj Karīm, the acknowledged leader of the group. Each of the principal rituals and activities involved in the pilgrimage process is treated in one of the "seven days": the evening meeting of the group in the village, the preparation of the baked food for the festival, the journey to Ṭanṭā, the hostelry where they stay, the big night of the festival itself, the farewell, and lastly the way, a term steeped in the lore of Islamic mysticism but here used to assess the impact of time and change on such traditional practices.

However, while this work may provide the most authentic, unsentimental and undoctrinaire account of an Egyptian village yet written in modern Arabic fiction, it also has other virtues of equal, if not more, significance. For the time period over which the descriptions of these seven stages are spread is at least fifteen years, and during that time 'Abd al-'Azīz grows up. As his education proceeds, his attitude to the village and, in particular, to his father and the group of dervishes, alters radically. Through this technique we are presented not only with vivid

[56] Cairo: Dār al-Kātib al-'Arabī, n.d. 1969? (= *Ayyām*).
[57] See Ṭāhā Badr, *al-Riwā'ī wa-al-arḍ*.

descriptions of life in both village and provincial city but also with a telling contrast between 'Abd al-'Azīz's present and past impressions of the annual events of the pilgrimage. Flashbacks at each stage record his feelings during younger days, and the entire sequence reveals an ever-increasing distaste for the entire underpinning of tradition upon which the rituals and ceremonies are built. Through the narrator's account of the changing attitudes of the boy to his village, his father, and the traditional values which are personified in the dervishes, we are given, in a mirror as it were, a kind of *Bildungsroman* in which the modern notions which 'Abd al-'Azīz acquires through his secondary schooling in Ṭanṭā and his university days in Alexandria are pitted against his love for his father and for the village where he grew up. Within this context, a touch of irony is provided by the fact that, whereas the city of Ṭanṭā represents the goal of the dervishes' aspirations during their pilgrimage to the shrine, for 'Abd al-'Azīz the very same city is the place to which he has gone for his secondary education. While he is there, he not only notices the significant differences between life in the city and in his own village, but learns as a part of the modern educational process certain things which call into question in his own mind the traditional attitudes and beliefs of his father and the dervish group. The entire novel may thus be seen as a view from within of a long and often difficult process of change, of the confrontation between the popular religion and superstition prevalent within the village structure and aspects of the changing world outside presented by city life and modern education.

The novel opens at sunset, and in its roseate hues we are immediately introduced to 'Abd al-'Azīz and his father. To the group of dervishes, al-Ḥājj Karīm is "their leader, while they love him, obey him and revere him". As a father, he is "good, beloved and awe-inspiring", and the little boy "snuggles up to his father like a tiny kitten, small and full of love".[58] The choice of sunset also provides a contrast with the heat and rigours of the day. As the group gathers in the evening at al-Ḥājj Karīm's house, we are introduced to them one by one through the eyes and ears of the boy: Aḥmad Badawī, Muḥammad Kāmil, Muḥammad "the dandy" (the local womaniser who is famous not only for his wife, Rawā'iḥ, who steals from everyone in the

[58] *Ayyām*, 7.

village, but also for his girl-friend, al-Gāziya); ʿAlī Khalīl, the owner of the general store, al-ʿIrāqī, the deaf-mute, ʿUmar Farḥūd, the camel driver, and Salīm al-Sharkasī, the carpenter. During the daytime, each of them pursues his own livelihood, facing challenges and adversities of different kinds and yelling at his women and children. But in the evening the whole atmosphere changes as the group gathers to listen to readings of texts such as the famous *Burda* poem of al-Būṣīrī and to perform the ritual of the *dhikr*. Through a variety of flashbacks and inserts we learn a variety of details concerning the nature of the beliefs of this group, particularly through the visit of the *shaykh* of their order to the village; in this case, the visit is described as a joyous and momentous occasion, in marked contrast to Ṭāhā Ḥusayn's description of a similar event in *al-Ayyām* (translated as *An Egyptian childhood*) several decades earlier.[59] The entire group goes to meet the *shaykh* at the railway station, a large gathering is held at ʿAlī Khalīl's house, an animal is slaughtered, and there is much ceremony. By now too, the news has come for which the group waits eagerly each year: the date for the annual pilgrimage to the shrine of al-Sayyid al-Badawī in Ṭanṭā has been set, and preparations must begin. To meet the expenses of those preparations, al-Ḥājj Karīm has to sell off a little more of his land to al-Mitwallī Ṣārūkh. Even the young ʿAbd al-ʿAzīz is alarmed by this continuing process whereby Ṣārūkh's land holdings become a little larger each year at the expense of his father, but he is comforted by the soothing words of his father, "We ourselves own nothing. We're merely guardians".[60]

This first chapter succeeds brilliantly in setting the stage for the rest of the novel. It establishes the feelings of awe and delight which the young boy has for his father and the group which he leads. At the same time, it introduces in an as yet uncritical fashion some of the problems which are to beset ʿAbd al-ʿAzīz later in the work. Moreover, it gives the reader a marvellously vivid picture of the village and its participation in the activities and rituals of the group.

The second chapter deals with the preparations for departure,

[59] *Ibid.*, 36. See also Ṭāhā Ḥusayn, *al-Ayyām* I, Cairo: Dār al-Maʿārif, 1944, 88 ff.; trans. E.H. Paxton, *An Egyptian childhood*, London: Routledge, 1932, 95 ff.

[60] *Ayyām*, 36.

and by focusing on "the baking" (the chapter's actual title), the author provides the reader with an entirely different outlook on the village, that of its womenfolk.[61] All the women of the village wish to be part of the preparation of the food for such a blessed purpose, and their conversations and gossiping in the kitchens of al-Ḥājj Karīm's house give us a further valuable dimension on the village as a whole and on the men whom we have met in the first chapter in particular. From ʿAbd al-ʿAzīz's viewpoint, the situation of this chapter is also used to advantage. That he is now older is shown convincingly by his awakening sexuality and by the way in which the girls are described. They seem relatively unaware of his presence, but he is certainly aware of them, as the nubile Ṣabāḥ finds out in a dark storeroom.[62] This proximity to the women of the village also implies—at least within the time frame of this chapter—a distance from his father. It is therefore significant that from the very beginning there are signs, albeit muted, of an emerging critical eye. This chapter opens with a description vastly different in impact from that of the first: ʿAbd al-ʿAzīz wakes up in the night in an overcrowded, stuffy room. As the chapter proceeds, we learn that al-Ḥājj Karīm has two wives, and the young boy's description of the second wife makes it clear that her status in the house is not a happy one. But above all, there is a none too flattering picture of the relationship of al-Ḥājj Karīm with ʿAbd al-ʿAzīz's mother:

> Long years went by without the two worlds ever coming together: that of al-Ḥājj Karīm which soared on wings of divine miracles and blessings ..., and that of his own mother which was limited to pots and pans and grain stores.[63]

While the young boy still retains earlier memories of bitter fights between his father and mother inside him "like the vestiges of a wound which festered", it is characteristic of this phase of the novel that the boy's chief regret is that his father is losing his fierceness towards her.

By the third chapter, the preparations are over and the day of departure has arrived. And, if there were signs of unease in ʿAbd al-ʿAzīz's thoughts in the second chapter, they have now

[61] In the first chapter, the women of the village remain very much in the background. See e.g. 37.

[62] *Ayyām*, 76.

[63] *Ibid.*, 53.

become considerably more explicit. He now sleeps on the roof in a move which is considerably more than a token gesture. The stuffy room which he described at the beginning of the second chapter is now a nightmarish vision, where "children are in heaps on the floor, a pile of nakedness, sweat and vile stench".[64] In this room of his is another cause of his increasing sense of separation, his books:

> ... his illness and cure, the words of which led him into weird mazes. There was nothing fixed in his life any more. The fiercesome cudgels of knowledge were smashing all his illusions one after another. They made him feel brazen and bitter, and the sharp pain of it all had him addicted.[65]

As the group of dervishes makes ready to depart, we are made to feel the contradictory emotions which are pulling ʿAbd al-ʿAzīz in different directions. He wants to go to Ṭanṭā with them, and yet he feels that

> his head is loaded down with uncontrollable question marks, while his heart is beset with an uninterrupted anxiety.[66]

As if to confirm these doubts, there is a most unflattering portait of the *shaykh* from Sharqiyya who had abandoned his studies at al-Azhar "without acquiring any learning at all".[67] But, in contrast to his, the arrival of ʿUmar Farḥūd's camel to load provisions for the journey provokes a reminiscence of earlier trips which is full of an affection for the village people and an admiration for his father's important position recalling the opening chapter. As the train departs for Ṭanṭā and ʿAbd al-ʿAzīz returns to the village, his thoughts are a mixture of a desire to travel and an intense feeling of affection for his father and the dervishes.[68]

The action of the fourth and fifth chapters is set in Ṭanṭā itself, and once again the author uses the possibilities of his approach to narrative point of view to best advantage. ʿAbd al-ʿAzīz is now going to school in Ṭanṭā, and the beginning of the fourth chapter ("The hostelry") finds him proceeding through the city towards the railway station in order to meet his father and the dervish group. This procedure affords ample oppor-

64 *Ibid.*, 83.
65 *Ibid.*
66 *Ibid.*, 91.
67 *Ibid.*, 92.
68 *Ibid.*, 111.

tunity for description of and comment on city life, not to mention remarks about the numbers of country peasants who are, like his father and the dervishes, flocking to the city for the festival. The occasion is not wasted, and the comparisons start at once. The village is said to be like a graveyard day and night, whereas the city is full of movement, orderly and clean.[69] As ʿAbd al-ʿAzīz makes his way to the station, he makes a point of describing those elements which illustrate the modernity of city life, the speeding cars and buses, the cinemas and the shops with all their wares on display. This detailed picture of the noisy, bustling city serves to make the boy's meeting with the dervishes at the station all the more awkward:

These men in their tatty clothes and red skull-caps, with their faces tanned by the sun and pock-marked by malnutrition ..., they were his relatives, his heart and eyes. ... How he wished they looked cleaner and bolder, not poor, stupid and afraid like this! In school he boasted about being a peasant in front of the city kids, but inside he felt angry and resentful. If only they weren't like this.[70]

This feeling obviously communicates itself to his father and his followers, for a sense of strain and distance is almost palpable between ʿAbd al-ʿAzīz and the men. And when he refuses to join them in their annual visit to the cinema, the extent of the gap separating the boy from his village origins becomes clear to everyone.

The fifth chapter describes the events of "the big night", and that is precisely what it is within the framework of the relationship between ʿAbd al-ʿAzīz and his father as well. It opens with the same kind of repulsive impression of the surroundings as occurs at the start of the third chapter. A greasy stew is being prepared for the large assembled company in the hostelry where they are staying. In addition to the smell of oil and grease, there is the overpowering stench of the lavatory, and ʿAbd al-ʿAzīz almost vomits in sheer revulsion.[71] As the tensions begin to mount inside him, he sits there "watching this human floor mat gnawing on its food ..., pouncing on it with a grotesque bestiality".[72] When his father

[69] *Ibid.*, 114.
[70] *Ibid.*, 126.
[71] *Ibid.*, 152.
[72] *Ibid.*, 157.

asks him to eat too, we have a forewarning of what is to come when the boy refuses point blank.

Unable to tolerate the atmosphere, both physical and mental, any longer, 'Abd al-'Azīz goes for a walk round the city. He visits the fair ground and is then drawn inexorably towards the mosque, wondering all the while if it is some deep-rooted influence of his father which is even now drawing him towards the shrine. When he returns to the hostelry, it is to find things exactly as they were when he left. In a devastating comparison, he compares the figure of his father standing in the middle of the assembly with the dying body of 'Antar, the hero of one of the mediaeval Arabic romances.[73] The stage is now set for the climax. With little or no warning, al-Ḥājj Karīm's son launches into a tirade against them:

> You're people with no sense, no brains. You meander about like animals, not knowing where you're going or where you've come from. ... What are you doing? Where are you going? Where have you come from? You stupid pagans![74]

While everyone is stunned, it is almost as though the boy's father has been expecting something of this sort. He issues a stinging rebuke to his son, tells him to leave, and calls him an unbeliever. Fortunately at this point, some of the men intervene with excuses and in any case the need for sleep draws a veil over the entire sorry scene. 'Abd al-'Azīz goes to the children's room and tries to sleep, even finding time to appreciate the body of Samīra, the girl whom he is supposed to marry. But his thoughts will not allow him any rest, and he goes out into the streets.

This climax is very similar in its impact to the destruction of the lamp in the mosque of Sayyida Zaynab about which we read in Yaḥyā Ḥaqqī's famous work, *Qindīl Umm Hāshim* (translated as *The saint's lamp*).[75] In that work too, Ismā'īl's destructive act is symbolic of an attack on Islam and, more particularly, popular religious beliefs within Islam. But whereas in Ḥaqqī's work the events which follow the challenge are intended to illustrate the possibilities of compromise and reconciliation, in Qāsim's work the relentless process of change allows for no

[73] *Ibid.*, 170.
[74] *Ibid.*, 171-2.
[75] Cairo: Dār al-Mā'ārif, 1944, 46; trans. Mustafa Badawi, Leiden: E.J. Brill, 1973, 29-30.

such developments. The sixth chapter is also set in Ṭanṭā like its two predecessors, thus forming a neat symmetry with the first three set in the village. But place in this chapter is of less importance than time. Called "The farewell", this chapter is not merely the end of one particular pilgrimage year but the final occasion on which the group will come to the city to perform the ceremonies. Muḥammad the Dandy's girl-friend, al-Gāziya, has died, and he himself is going blind. Both Muḥammad Kāmil and Salīm al-Sharkasī leave before all the ceremonies are over, and this leads al-Ḥājj Karīm to acknowledge that the men in his group have changed and that his own hold on them is weakening.[76] This same force of change is also having its effects on the young girls of Ṭanṭā and the very streets of the city itself.[77]

With these circumstances in mind, it is a forlorn group which makes the final visit to the mosque. ʿAbd al-ʿAzīz goes with them, but his motivations are those of pity and concern for his aging and ailing father. His emotions are succinctly expressed:

He was baffled and alone. Nothing could move his heart, even though he was there with them. Cold and lifeless. He kept looking round him in embarrassment. ... He gave a sad smile, one which bade farewell to the joys, the profound joys of childhood.[78]

The chapter ends as they watch the demolition of the fair-ground which ʿAbd al-ʿAzīz had visited the "day" before.

The beginning of the seventh chapter finds ʿAbd al-ʿAzīz hurrying home from Alexandria where he is at university. He has received an unspecific message that his father is very ill. In fact, al-Ḥājj Karīm has had a severe heart attack while endeavouring to raise some money and now needs medical attention and drugs which the family cannot afford. ʿAbd al-ʿAziz's return to his village also serves to show that the changes which have been illustrated in previous chapters through life in the city are now influencing life in the village as well. ʿAlī Khalīl, the owner of the general store, has died, and Muḥammad the Dandy is now completely blind. ʿAbd al-ʿAzīz takes the family's water-buffalo out to turn the water-wheel and irrigate their vastly diminished land. When the animal collapses

[76] *Ayyām*, 183.
[77] *Ibid.*, 179, 194.
[78] *Ibid.*, 189, 191.

and has to be disposed of, he sees a further aspect of this change:

These were not his father's men. They had a severe look about them and laughed loudly. When they sat down together in the afternoon, it wasn't for nice conversation; they listened to the news on the radio and made vigorous comments. They all seemed bitter, rash and stern.[79]

As the decision is made to cut the animal up with minimal compensation to al-Ḥājj Karīm's family, ʿAbd al-ʿAzīz reflects ruefully on the reticence of al-Sharkasī the carpenter and Aḥmad Badawī, two of his father's erstwhile companions, who watch the entire process from the sidelines. But he comes to realise that they, like his father, belong to a past generation and that their mode of doing business with each other has disappeared, along with their entire system of values and beliefs. As ʿAbd al-ʿAzīz contemplates the state of affairs of his family and the village, it is Samīra, the girl whom he was supposed to marry but who is now married to someone else, the same Samīra who gave him a few moments' comfort after his blazing row with his father in Ṭanṭā, who lightens his depression.[80] When he leaves her, it is to go to the local café where he finds himself drawn with a strange naturalness into the intense discussions of politics fuelled by the news broadcasts on the radio:

In his heart he felt like one of them. There was the same bitterness, anger and pain. The sweat poured from his forehead as he kept shouting out words and phrases ...[81]

In the above analytical description of *Ayyām al-insān al-sabʿa* we have followed the format of the work itself, but it is hoped that illustrations from the text and comments on certain aspects of technique will have already shown that this novel is written with a great deal of skill.

The first area in which this skill is apparent is in the description of the environment. The phrase "local colour" is perhaps an overworked one, but that is precisely what Qāsim manages to convey in this novel to a degree beyond that of any other Egyptian novel devoted to life in the countryside. This is

[79] *Ibid.*, 220.
[80] *Ibid.*, 230-3.
[81] *Ibid.*, 235.

achieved in a number of ways. In the first place, the surroundings are allowed to emerge from within the framework of the narrative about the dervish group in a manner which is entirely deceptive in its spontaneity; as any writer of fiction knows, such spontaneity is only achieved as the result of a great deal of narrative craft. Furthermore, the author does not appear to force upon the environment or the structure of the narrative any personal or political agenda. It is obvious that Qāsim is intimately familiar with the surroundings which he describes, something which can be easily documented;[82] but the peasants and the village in which they live are not turned into overt symbols of larger political or social theories. A further feature which undoubtedly lends realism to the environment is the author's use of language. We refer here not only to the generous use of the colloquial dialect of the Delta,[83] but the way in which interior monologues and even the more narrative passages reflect very much the spontaneous language of speech: the short phrases, the conspicuous lack of connection between different utterances, and the adventurous use of tenses to heighten the impact of the narrative.

These last comments have brought us to the question of style, about which a further comment needs to be made; specifically, the author's use of the most picturesque phrases to describe people and objects. A few examples will have to suffice. In the description of the city of Ṭanṭā, the vendors are pictured as "working with both their hands and mouths, a bundle of nerves obsessed with movement and noise". A peasant from the village who now lives in the city is said to have "eyes, two reddened cavities which looked like pigeons' anuses". Again in Ṭanṭā, the room is described in part in the following fashion:

> The lanterns were hot moons, stretching out flaming antennae like gleaming cockroaches and scorching people's faces. The pictures hanging by nails from the walls seemed like faded eyeballs looking down on the proceedings with a questioning gaze which was silent and stupid.[84]

[82] See *al-Ṭalīʿa* (Sept. 1970), 21-2.

[83] I must acknowledge here my thanks to Professor Joseph Bell of the State University of New York at Binghamton who allowed me to peruse his translation of Qāsim's work (as yet unpublished), a version which has benefited greatly from the opportunity to consult with the author on a number of matters relating to the text of the novel.

[84] *Ayyām*, 117, 134, 156.

At the beginning of the discussion of this novel we noted the way in which the succession of chapters was used not only to show the events of the pilgrimage to Ṭanṭā but also to reflect the upbringing and education of ʿAbd al-ʿAzīz, the lens through which the reader sees the characters and events of the story. When we realise that Qāsim himself was born in a village, went to school in Ṭanṭā and to university in Alexandria, the close association of author and narrator should come as no surprise.[85] While this close identification produces positive results in the main, there does appear to be one aspect from which the use of ʿAbd al-ʿAzīz as "narrative lens" leads to an unsatisfactory result. The picture of the village which we receive in the early chapters of the novel is, as we have noted, that of the young son of al-Ḥājj Karīm. It gains its authenticity from the perspective which he provides but, by the same token, it is restricted to those aspects which concern him both as a boy of his particular age and as the son of his particular family. Other aspects of village life are not discussed. Thus, when we are presented in the final chapters with a different picture of the village, still seen through the eyes of ʿAbd al-ʿAzīz but this time as an "outsider" returning from the University of Alexandria, we wonder whether the changes which have occurred can really have happened so fast. This impression is further emphasised by the careful way in which changes in city life have been portrayed in the previous chapters set in Ṭanṭā. The reader is left to wonder at the end of the work whether the changes which confront ʿAbd al-ʿAzīz in the final chapter have not been taking place throughout the narrative, but he has been either too young or preoccupied to notice them.

However, even if we acknowledge the possibility of this inconsistency, *Ayyām al-insān al-sabʿa* presents the reader with a memorable portrait of Egyptian village society and some of the characters who populate it, and at the same time poses to us in a spontaneous and totally attractive fashion some of the larger issues of change, the impact of which is not confined to the countryside of Egypt.

5. *Mawsim al-hijra ilā al-shamāl*
al-Ṭayyib Ṣāliḥ

Al-Ṭayyib Ṣāliḥ's novel *Mawsim al-hijra ilā al-shamāl* ("Season

[85] *al-Ṭalīʿa, loc. cit.*

of migration to the North") is one of several works in modern Arabic literature which deal with the meeting of Middle Eastern and Western cultures, and particularly with the confrontation between traditional and modern values when a Middle Eastern character in a novel spends some time in the West as part of his or her education—a novel of upbringing or *Bildungsroman*, to use the German term.[86] In this case, one of the two major characters is Muṣṭafā Saʿīd, a young Sudanese student whose brilliant career at school in the Sudan and Cairo is capped by a period spent studying and then teaching in England. The means by which this meeting or confrontation between East and West (or between North and South, as expressed in the novel) is that of Muṣṭafā's relationships with a number of English women. However, whereas the character of Mary in Yaḥyā Ḥaqqī's *Qindīl Umm Hāshim* succeeds in totally demolishing the traditional values of Ismāʿīl the Egyptian before building up some new ones and then abandoning him to his own devices,[87] Muṣṭafā Saʿīd in Ṣāliḥ's novel comes "as a conqueror", "the invader who had come from the South, and this was the icy battlefield from which I would not make a safe return".[88] His love affairs with three women, Ann Hammond, an Oxford undergraduate, Sheila Greenwood, a Soho waitress, and Isabella Seymour, an older married woman who, we discover later, is dying of cancer,[89] are all bitter-sweet episodes which end in the suicide of the girl concerned. However, one of the women, Jean Morris, does not succumb to the mysterious and vicious allures of Muṣṭafā but instead, succeeds in attracting him through her own outrageous conduct and taunts him to such a degree that he marries her. As Muṣṭafā Saʿīd says later, however, "I was the pirate sailor and Jean Morris the shore of destruction".[90] Their love-hate relationship reaches the point that in a moment of almost ritual (and indeed sexual) violence

[86] Beirut: Dār al-ʿAwda, 1969. trans. Denys Johnson-Davies, *Season of migration to the North*, London: Heinemann, 1969. Al-Ṭayyib Ṣāliḥ was born in the Sudan in 1929 and studied at the University of Khartum before travelling to England, where he studied at the University of London. He has also worked for the BBC.

[87] See the recent perceptive study by Susan A. Gohlman, "Women as cultural symbols in Yaḥyā Ḥaqqī's *Saint's Lamp*", *JAL* X (1979), 117-27.

[88] *Mawsim*, 63, 162; trans., 60, 160.

[89] *Ibid.*, 142; trans., 141.

[90] *Ibid.*, 162; trans., 160.

he murders her. Even as he listens at his trial to the words of one of his former teachers describing his brilliant career, Muṣṭafā Sa'īd displays some of the internal complexities of his stance:

"It was I who killed them. I am a desert of thirst. I am no Othello. I am a lie. Why don't you sentence me to be hanged and so kill the lie?" But Professor Foster-Keen turned the trial into a conflict between two worlds, a struggle of which I was one of the victims.[91]

However, these remarks which Mustafā Sa'īd finds so unpalatable and hypocritical[92] manage to secure him a relatively light prison sentence of seven years for the murder of his wife. Thereafter, he returns to his native Sudan after some travels and settles in a village on the Nile.

The preceding description may give the impression that this novel has an obvious hero and focal point, Muṣṭafā Sa'īd, the brilliant Sudanese student with "a mind like a knife",[93] who goes to England, the very source of that society which had dominated his homeland for so long.[93] This impression is both deceptive and at the same time a mark of the brilliant way in which this novel is constructed. In fact, Muṣṭafā Sa'īd's narrative occupies a relatively small portion of the work.[95] Surrounding this section is the frame of yet another story, that of the Narrator, another Sudanese student who also goes to England for seven years to earn a degree in English literature and then returns to become at first a teacher of Arabic literature and then an Inspector of Education. Muṣṭafā Sa'īd has taken up residence in the narrator's village during his absence. The part of the novel before Muṣṭafā's own narrative is therefore taken up with the Narrator's gradual introduction to the new member of the village society. To the Narrator's astonishment, he hears Muṣṭafā reciting English poetry one night, and eventually succeeds in persuading the reluctant Muṣṭafā to tell him his story. Immediately following Muṣṭafā's narrative, the Narrator returns to his narrative function: from Khartum where he is carrying out his educational duties he learns that Muṣṭafā Sa'īd has been drowned in the river. The Narrator hurries back to the

[91] *Ibid.*, 37; trans., 33.
[92] *Ibid.*, 96-7; trans., 93.
[93] *Ibid.*, 26; trans., 22.
[94] *Ibid.*, 56-7; trans., 53.
[95] *Ibid.*, 23-48; trans., 19-44.

village to discover that Muṣṭafā had made elaborate preparations for what appears to be his suicide and that he has made the Narrator the guardian of his wife and two children.

This places the Narrator in a complex position within the closely-knit structure of the village. He is a bachelor, and Muṣṭafā's widow is still young. Several suggestions are made to him on the subject, but he does not make the final step. Meanwhile, Wād Rayyis, the village's most prominent womaniser, who believes that women are on earth entirely to please men,[96] sets his heart on marrying the widow. Even though she tells the Narrator that she will kill herself if the marriage takes place, things are allowed to proceed. Yet again, the Narrator is called back to the village to hear the grisly tale of the death of both Wād Rayyis and his new wife, Muṣṭafā's widow: she has refused to consort with him for a long time, and Wād Rayyis finally decides to take her. After a gruesome struggle she kills him and then herself. Only Bint Maḥjūb, an earthy widow of the village, can summon the necessary courage to tell the Narrator of this event, the shame of which is shared by the entire village. This event finally spurs the Narrator into investigating the one room in Muṣṭafā's house which no-one else has entered since his death. Here the Narrator finds all kinds of echoes from Muṣṭafā's past life in England, letters from his girl-friends, a huge library of European books and other memorabilia. These echoes are able to fill in many details of Muṣṭafā's narrative earlier in the novel, while the existence of such a perfect replica of the English scholar-gentleman's study in a remote village on the banks of the Nile in the Sudan points up the many tensions reflected in the life of Muṣṭafā Saʿīd. It is, in a word, a perfect symbol of his alienation from the native land whose identity he had sought to assert during his time in London.

This section finishes with the graphic description of Jean Morris's murder, as the Narrator reads from diaries of Muṣṭafā regarding his tortured existence with her.[97] The very next page transfers us back to the Narrator, and in a stunning contrast we are moved from a bed in London at some point in the past to the Nile at the close of the events in the novel: the Narrator, apparently overwhelmed by the horrifying death of the widow

[96] *Ibid.*, 87 ff.; trans., 83 ff.
[97] *Ibid.*, 157 ff.; trans., 155 ff.

whose guardian he was and by the situation in the village, follows Muṣṭafā's footsteps into the Nile. However, there is a crucial difference; as the Narrator tells us:

All my life I had not chosen, had not decided. Now I am making a decision. I choose life. I shall live because there are a few people I want to stay with for the longest possible time and because I have duties to discharge.[98]

The novel ends with his calls for help as the river swirls around him.

This brief account of this work already shows the superb way in which the theme of contact between East and West is handled and how rich is the depiction of the clash of characters and cultures. However, the author not only succeeds in handling the complex time frame of the narrative with great skill, but also manages to sprinkle into the various sections a number of clues which call into question the separation which can be made on a purely realistic level between the characters of Muṣṭafā Saʿīd and the Narrator. The author may even be said to tantalise us by trying to place the Narrator at a distance from the life and career of Muṣṭafā Saʿīd, by incorporating Muṣṭafā Saʿīd's own narration as a separate unit, within the larger "frame" structure.

However, the clues continue to assert themselves throughout the work: we have already cited Muṣṭafā's thoughts about himself as he listens to the evidence at his own trial; to this can be added a comment of the Narrator's:

A disturbing thought occurs to me that Muṣṭafā Saʿīd never happened, that he was in fact a lie, a phantom, a dream or a nightmare; that he had come to the people of that village one suffocatingly dark night, and when they opened their eyes to the sunlight he was nowhere to be seen...[99]

The link between the two characters is suggested in early parts of the novel,[100] but the reader finds himself confronted by it when the Narrator finally enters Muṣṭafā's study. "My adversary is within", he says at first, "and I needs must confront him", but, once in the room, the link is firmly established:

[98] *Ibid.*, 170; trans., 168.
[99] *Ibid.*, 50; trans., 46.
[100] For example, "Was it likely that what has happened to Muṣṭafā Saʿīd could have happened to me? He had said that he was a lie, so was I also a lie?" (*ibid.*, 52; trans., 49).

... Out of the darkness there emerged a frowning face with pursed lips that I knew but could not place. I moved towards it with hate in my heart. It was Muṣṭafā Sa'īd. The face grew a neck, the neck two shoulders and a chest, then a trunk and two legs, and I found myself standing face-to-face with myself. This is not Muṣṭafā Sa'īd—it's a picture of me frowning at my face from a mirror. Suddenly the picture disappeared, and I sat in the darkness for I know not how long listening intently and hearing nothing.[101]

These passages serve to make it quite clear that beneath the surface level of description in this work there lies a psychological stratum which is sometimes, but not always, visible. Al-Ṭayyib Ṣāliḥ has stated that at the time of writing this work he was much influenced by the writings of Freud,[102] and the whole subject is explored most convincingly by Muḥammad Ṣiddīq in a recent article, where he also points out the remarkable detachment which characterises Muṣṭafā's relationship with his widowed mother and the effect which that may have had on his attitudes towards women later in life.[103]

Whether we interpret this kind of analysis as suggesting that Muṣṭafā Sa'īd is a representative of the Narrator's subconscious or whether we choose to treat them as separate individuals, the fact remains that the final pages of the novel show clearly that Muṣṭafā Sa'īd and his story have had a profound effect on the Narrator. The tensions involved in Muṣṭafā's adoption of Western culture and in his vicious confrontation with those who live within it have led to his eventual demise. The responsibilities thrust on the Narrator by that demise and the consequences thereof lead him to a new resolution, one which may involve a compromise between extremes, something which does not seem to have been part of Muṣṭafā's make-up:

It is not my concern whether or not life has meaning. If I am unable to forgive, then I shall try to forget. I shall live by force and cunning.[104]

It is at this point that the Narrator starts struggling in the Nile water and calling for help; and so the novel ends.

The above discussion of the narrative structure of this work

[101] *Ibid.*, 135-6; trans., 134-5.

[102] *al-Ṭayyib Ṣāliḥ 'abqarī al-riwāya al-'Arabiyya*, ed. Aḥmad Sa'īd Muḥammadiyya *et al.*, Beirut: Dār al-'Awda, 1976, 215.

[103] "The process of individuation in al-Tayyeb Salih's novel *Season of migration to the North*", *JAL* IX (1978), 67-104, esp. 70 ff.

[104] *Mawsim*, 171; trans., 168-9.

has inevitably included some reference to the treatment of time, particularly on the larger scale, through the fragmentation of chronological sequence and the use of flashback. On a more detailed stylistic level, we should draw attention to the constant shifting between past, present and, occasionally, future, which is to be found throughout the work; the following is just one example:

> I had loafed around the streets of Cairo, visited the opera, gone to the theatre, and once I had swum across the Nile. Nothing whatsoever had happened except that the waterskin had distended further, the bowstring had become more taut. The arrow will shoot forth towards other unknown horizons.[105]

This process of switching between the different time frames is most effective in showing the way in which the tension implicit in the memories of the past is constantly impinging on the present in the consciousness of Muṣṭafā Saʿīd and the Narrator whom he has chosen as guardian of his family and heritage.

The above quotation also illustrates another feature of al-Ṭayyib Ṣāliḥ's novelistic technique, namely his use of imagery in order to heighten the impact of the cultural confrontation. The bow and arrow is just one of the more pointed images, as it were, used to describe Muṣṭafā's callous and defiant stance; it will be remembered that as a young man he was said to have a mind like a knife.[106] In the description of Muṣṭafā Saʿīd's exploits, the imagery of the desert, obvious sexual allusions and figures from history and lore of East and West, the climbing of the mountain peak, the driving of a tent peg into the soil, the entry of Lord Carnarvon into the tomb of Tutankhamun, Shahrayār and Shahrāzād, Othello, camels and caravans, all these contribute to the portrayal of this complex individual in his eventually unsuccessful quest to come to terms with his destiny.

When *Season of migration to the North* first appeared in 1967, it was greeted with wonderment by a number of distinguished literary critics, including Rajāʾ al-Naqqāsh and ʿAlī al-Rāʿī. A book containing a selection of critical articles on the work describes Ṣāliḥ as "the genius of the modern Arabic novel" in its title. These few pages have only been able to draw attention

[105] *Ibid.*, 32; trans., 28. See also *Mawsim*, 60, 108; trans., 57, 105.
[106] *Ibid.*, 31, 37 and 26, 33, 35; trans., 27, 33 and 22, 29, 31.

to some of the major features of this work which seems destined to become a classic of Arabic fiction.

6. *Al-Safīna*
Jabrā Ibrāhīm Jabrā

"The sea is the bridge to salvation". That is the way in which the Palestinian novelist, poet, critic and artist, Jabrā Ibrāhīm Jabrā, begins his brilliant novel *al-Safīna* ("The ship", 1969). It is surely one of the intentional ironies of this work that, while present time is set during a cruise on the Mediterranean, the real theme of this work has nothing to do with the sea but rather with the land, land as history, land as responsibility, land as aspiration for the future. This is most clearly seen in the two principal narrators of the work: ʿIṣām Salmān and Wadīʿ ʿAssāf. ʿIṣām Salmān, the architect from Baghdad, is running away from land, the land which his family owns in Iraq, the land for which his father had killed another man, thus condemning himself to a lifelong exile away from his homeland and family and condemning ʿIṣām to a childhood and adolescence under the control of a determined mother. But above all, ʿIṣām is running away from Lumā, the beautiful and intelligent girl whom he has met while studying in England and who, fatefully, turns out to be related to the man whom his father has killed.[107] Thus, although they are in love, the so-called "tribalism" of Iraqi society has ruled out any prospect of marriage. Somewhat in desperation, Lumā has embarked on a marriage of societal convenience with Fāliḥ ʿAbd al-Ḥasīb, a brilliant surgeon, moody, morose and always looking for specific answers to every question without finding them. The other narrator is Wadīʿ ʿAssāf, the Palestinian businessman living out his exile from his homeland in Kuwait. He is running towards the land, his own property in Jerusalem for which he and his martyred friend, Fāyiz, fought in vain in 1948. This quest of Wadīʿ's remains, of course, an aspiration (as it does for many other Palestinians), but that does not diminish the ardour with which he pursues it or with which he tries to persuade his girl-friend, Mahā al-Ḥājj, to join him, thus abandoning her home and medical career in Beirut.

When these and other characters board the *Hercules*, the

[107] *al-Safina*, Beirut: Dār al-Nahār, 1970, 229.

Greek cruise ship, in Beirut, their meeting seems to be purely coincidental. ʿIṣām's reaction, for example, on seeing Lumā with her husband can be imagined, and the agony of being so near and yet so far from the woman he loves is only made worse by the fact that his cabin is next to theirs; through the thin dividing wall he even hears them making love on the bed in their cabin.[108] It emerges however that chance has nothing to do with this encounter. ʿIṣām has unwittingly set the process in motion by deciding to travel to Europe by boat. Lumā, eager to renew her affair with him, has discovered this fact and booked a passage on the same voyage for herself and her husband. Little does she realise that, while she is arranging things to suit her convenience, her husband Fāliḥ proceeds to do exactly the same. During the course of a medical conference in Beirut, he has met Mahā al-Ḥājj, Wadīʿ ʿAssāf's girl-friend, and her friend, the Italian Emilia Farnesi. Fāliḥ and Emilia have fallen in love. Thus, when Fāliḥ suggests to Emilia that she join the cruise, she books a passage for herself and encourages Mahā to come along with Wadīʿ. Just before the cruise, Mahā and Wadīʿ have one of their periodic quarrels and she refuses to come on the cruise. Wadīʿ therefore boards the boat alone.

This then is the complex and explosive web of characters and relationships as the novel begins. The narrative present which forms one time frame for the novel consists of the week-long cruise on the ship, during which it sails from Beirut to Athens, through the Corinth Canal, round the south coast of Italy through the Straits of Messina to Naples.[109] Within this time, a few events happen. A Dutchman attempts to commit suicide by throwing himself off the boat in the Gulf of Corinth; he is unsuccessful in his attempt, but the event itself serves in retrospect as a premonition, particularly in view of the comments which are made by several of the characters at the time.[110] Later that same evening, Lumā dances on the deck to the music of Umm Kulthūm's singing, and the eyes of everyone are rivetted on the gorgeous Iraqi beauty. It is this event which triggers her husband's fateful decision; in his own words:

Your dance last night was my death sentence. It helped me reach my

108 *Ibid.*, 14.

109 The question of the treatment of time in *al-Safīna* is covered by Ḍiyā' al-Sharqāwī in *al-Maʿrifa* 193-4 (March-April 1978), 7 ff.

110 *al-Safīna*, 96 ff.

final decision. I could have killed you yesterday. I don't know how I put up with it, how I listened to my better judgement and decided not to do it.[111]

A third drama unfolds when Maḥmūd al-Rāshid, a teacher of political science on his way to teach at Lille University, goes berserk at the sight of one of the seamen on the boat and claims that it is the man who tortured him in jail. To prove his point, he strips off his shirt and reveals that his back is indeed covered with the most gruesome scars. This episode shakes even the artificial tranquility of the group, but the Captain of the vessel brushes the whole thing off as a minor problem. He is faced by something more pressing, the onset of a major storm which rocks the boat for a whole day. This serves to bring Fāliḥ and Emilia together as the only passengers (along with Wadīʿ) who are not seasick, the fate which unites ʿIṣām and Lumā in misery. It is during this episode that Wadīʿ comes to realise that Emilia and Fāliḥ are lovers.[112]

When the boat reaches Naples, a trip to Capri is suggested. Although elaborate arrangements are made, neither Fāliḥ, Lumā, Emilia nor ʿIṣām go; they have all decided to make use of the involvement of the others in the trip to Capri to spend a few precious hours with their real beloved in Naples. Lumā and ʿIṣām spend a blissful day in the city, during the course of which they are seen by Emilia and Fāliḥ who have booked into a hotel. Emilia is hard put to it to arouse the interest of Fāliḥ, who has become more and more morose, and the scene in the hotel bedroom when she tries every ruse she knows to get him to make love to her is almost gothic in its sinister undertones of utter despair and frenzy. In something akin to a comedy of errors, everyone thinks that they have to get back to the boat before the Capri trippers return, and so the day is short. Feeling disconsolate after saying farewell to their lovers, ʿIṣām and Emilia turn round and go back to Naples for the evening. When they return late that night, Lumā is waiting for ʿIṣām, furious that he could go out with Emilia so soon after leaving her. They make passionate love in his cabin while Fāliḥ sleeps soundly next door. When she finally returns to her own cabin, it is only to return in a panic a few moments later; the somnolent Fāliḥ is

111 *Ibid.*, 222.
112 *Ibid.*, 151.

in fact dead, and has been for a while in a suicide executed with all the care and finesse of a surgeon. On the table where the empty bottle of pills lies is also a set of instructions and a will which has obviously been in preparation for some time. This is the dénouement indeed, and in its wake reality has to be faced in all its ruthless clarity. It is into this horrific situation that Mahā al-Ḥājj, Wadī''s girl-friend, now comes, having decided that her love for him is her overriding priority.

We mentioned earlier that present time—as just summarised—is not in and of itself the most significant feature of the narrative element in this novel. Throughout the work the events and surroundings trigger a whole series of flashbacks which allow the past to impinge on the present. Thus the use of two narrators (and Emilia Farnesi who recounts the episode with Fāliḥ in Naples) not only allows for the unfolding of the events of the cruise in chronological sequence and for the portrayal of the various characters from different points of view, but also enables the past to interpret and affect the present almost till the end of the novel. When Wadī' is told of the way in which Lumā originally booked the passage, thus setting off the entire train of events, he is still unable to believe that it actually happened that way.[113]

These flashbacks serve to fill in many necessary details concerning the upbringing, education and attitudes of the characters. 'Iṣām's first sight of Lumā in the opening chapter sets off a memory of their earlier times together in Baghdad, while the passage of the boat through the Corinth Canal to the music of Bach sends Wadī' back on a long journey into his past, to the feast of Christmas in Palestine, and to his boyhood friend, Fāyiz 'Aṭā'allāh (Atallah). This is followed by a long and vivid account of the fighting for Jerusalem in 1948 and the death of Fāyiz. At this point, it is worth observing that the description of Fāyiz's house in *The ship* is almost identical to Jabrā's description of his own home in Jerusalem to be found in his collection of articles, *al-Riḥla al-thāmina*.[114] The additional fact that Jabrā also lost a friend named 'Aṭā'allāh in the 1948 fighting and that in the novel both Fāyiz and Wadī' share Jabrā's own passion for painting lend even further emphasis to the loving detail and

[113] *Ibid.*, 230-1.

[114] *Ibid.*, 58. See also Jabrā, "al-Quds: al-zaman al-mujassad", in *al-Riḥla al-thāmina*, 107-8, and *Journal of Palestine Studies* VIII/2 (Winter 1979), 84.

intensity with which the author's hometown and the tragedy which has beset it in modern times are described in Wadī''s long flashback.

Other incidents recalled by the characters provide the reader with insights into their personality and, in some cases, premonitions of what is to come. Maḥmūd, for example, describes an incident as a boy at school when one of his school-friends does not reveal Maḥmūd as the real culprit and takes his punishment for him, saying afterwards that he hopes Maḥmūd will do the same for him one day. As Maḥmūd observes to the company in a manner which seems almost casual in the light of his crisis later on, he has been tortured many times since but has never implicated anybody, a revelation which, incidentally, introduces the theme of political oppression in the modern Arab world into an environment where cultural alienation seems to occupy the centre of the stage.[115]

When Lumā and 'Iṣām are finally alone together in Naples, they discuss the hopelessness of their situation, and the whole process brings the history of their love back into the consciousness of 'Iṣām: its blossoming and fruition in England where they were both studying, and its strangulation at the hands of "tribalism" in Iraq. All of which leads to the most important flashback of all, that of Fāliḥ in his death-note, although in this case the impact is on the living who remain behind and not on Fāliḥ himself. As 'Iṣām the narrator notes, it is a carefully prepared document and has been edited by its writer. To the background of Hamlet's question, "To be or not to be", Fāliḥ expresses his frustrations at being unable to find answers to questions: why did he fail to save the life of a seventeen year-old girl, while a seventy year-old man lived? How appropriate, too, that the author whose descriptive technique he cites should be Kafka.[116] He tells Lumā of his love for Emilia and forgives her for her own conduct; in conclusion, he discusses his own depression:

I spent my entire life searching for crises and revolutions such as these. Yet my humanity was always rejectionist, because it was maimed, disfigured, crushed from within and without. I reject the age of murder, the age of frustration. I reject despair. And now at last I

[115] *al-Safīna*, 115-16.
[116] *Ibid.*, 217.

reject hope. I wanted to rise above human beings, their concerns, their wretchedness and their cruelty, but I have failed.[117]

And, with Fāliḥ gone, many things are clarified. For Emilia, of course, all is lost. ʿIṣām is determined to accompany Lumā back to Baghdad where they will, of course, still face the same societal problems which have kept them apart before. Wadīʿ and Mahā are now happily united, but the return to Jerusalem and the land of Palestine is still a long way off. At the conclusion of the novel, therefore, the numerous problems which had been facing the characters can hardly be said to be resolved. As the two couples leave the ship, Wadīʿ is comforted to notice Maḥmūd standing a short distance behind Emilia; and when they have taken rooms in a hotel for the night, ʿIṣām observes in a concluding comment that, since it is midnight, they must have just finished dancing on board the ship.[118]

With this immensely rich blend of the past and present, Jabrā has fashioned one of the most brilliant and technically-satisfying novels yet to be written in Arabic. To the mastery of narrative point of view and the use of fractured time which have, I hope, been amply demonstrated in the preceding analysis, should be added a copious use of symbols. The sea and the ship are, of course, two of these; the ship provides a microcosm within which this collection of Arab intellectuals rehearse many of the issues affecting themselves, their people, and humanity in general, while the sea may, as in the Gulf of Corinth, provide a serene backdrop to this activity, or else, as in the day of the storm, set the scene in an atmosphere of disruption and nausea. In the case of Wadīʿ, a number of evocative images are formed through the use of Christian symbols, the church, the cave of Christ's birth, the candles, the chanting, and so on; in the particular case of Fāyiz, the association with John the Baptist is particularly effective.[119] These symbols and other allusions illustrate another aspect of Jabrā's artistry, namely his own immense knowledge of Western culture. *The ship* is full of discussions of works of literature (including Anatole France, Goethe, Dostoevsky, Camus and Kafka), works of music, painting and architecture, and references to myths and legends. The entire creation is

[117] *Ibid.*, 224.
[118] *Ibid.*, 243.
[119] *Ibid.*, 56.

couched in a style which rises above mere descriptive prose and often achieves the status of prose poetry. In fact, the work does contain poetry by Jabrā as well as quotations from other Arab poets, but it is not to these passages that I am referring in commenting on Jabrā's style in this way. Consider, for example, the opening paragraph of the novel which is so beautiful and appropriate that it is worth quoting in full:

> The sea is a bridge to salvation—the soft, the hoary, the compassionate sea. Today it has regained its vitality. The crash of its waves is a violent rhythm for the sap that sprays the face of heaven with flowers, large lips, and arms reaching out like alluring snares. Yes, the sea is a new salvation. Off to the West! To the agate isles! To the shore where the goddess of love emerged from the foam of the waves and the exhalations of the breeze.[120]

This is indeed a truly remarkable passage, which not only illustrates the use of language, but also the way in which the sea is treated as a symbol.

Escape, exile, loneliness, suicide, alienation, Palestine, the angst of the modern intellectual and particularly the Arab intellectual, these are the major themes which Jabrā explores with such artistry in this remarkable novel.

7. "Quartet"
Ismāʿīl Fahd Ismāʿīl

Kānat al-samā' zarqā' ("The sky was blue", n.d.)
al-Mustanqaʿāt al-ḍaw'iyya ("The light-swamps", 1971)
al-Ḥabl ("The rope", n.d.)
al-Ḍifāf al-ukhrā ("Other shores", 1973)

"This poet novelist", says the Egyptian colloquial poet, ʿAbd al-Raḥmān al-Abnūdī, "sorrowful, forceful and well-versed in our problems, has succeeded in blending his own public and private experiences in a way which is incredibly simple and spontaneous".[121] Behind any such simplicity and spontaneity there is always the work of a literary craftsman, and that is certainly the case here. Ismāʿīl's four novels may represent one of the most ambitious projects yet undertaken in the tradition of the contemporary Arabic novel, and it must be admitted at the outset that the result is only partially successful.

[120] *Ibid.*, 9.
[121] See the back cover of *Kānat al-samā' zarqā'*, Beirut: Dār al-ʿAwda, n.d.

However, that should in no way be allowed to detract from the considerable merits of individual novels in the group, most particularly in specific aspects of technique; of those we would single out the treatment of time, together with the investigation of the different levels of consciousness in the major character who is the focus of attention in each of the first three novels.

This last comment reveals a feature of the overall structuring of the work as a whole. The author himself describes the process with that same deceptive simplicity which was noted above:

Kānat al-samā' zarqā', *al-Mustanqa'āt al-ḍaw'iyya*, and *al-Ḥabl* are three short novels. *Al-Ḍifāf al-ukhrā* is an attempt to follow up on some of the characters in the previous three works within a single developing sequence of time.[122]

The particular time-frame within which this series of novels is set is that of Iraq in the 1960s. The author tells us as much in a published comment on the work, and while that should not be our only guide, there are sufficient historical references in the text to confirm his setting; no doubt, Iraqi readers can find even more specific allusions within the sequence of events and statements of the characters. In any case, this period emerges as a gruesome one for many elements of Iraqi society. Few writers have spoken of the atmosphere of this era with such eloquence and emotion as Badr Shākir al-Sayyāb in his poem *Madīnat al-Sindbād* ("City of Sindbad"):

There is death in the streets,
and barrenness in the fields,
and all that we love is dying.
They have bound up the water in the houses
And brooks are panting in the drought.
Behold, the Tatars have advanced,
Their knives are bleeding,
And our sun is blood, our food
is blood upon the platter.[123]

Within the world of Ismā'īl's quartet of novels, the societal conditions to which Sayyāb alludes above with such obvious

[122] "Kalimatun", *al-Ḍifāf al-ukhrā*, Beirut: Dār al-'Awda, 1973, 7.

[123] *Dīwān*, Beirut: Dār al-'Awda, 1971, 467; translated as "City of Sindbad" in *An anthology of modern Arabic poetry*, trans. Mounah A. Khouri and Hamid Algar, Berkeley: University of California Press, 97.

passion are—almost horrifyingly— implicit. Each character is revealed in the attempt to cope with these conditions, thus telling us a great deal about his own attitudes towards society and change. The final novel attempts to gather up some of the unresolved questions from the other three and to provide resolutions for them.

Kānat al-samā' zarqā' was written, the author tells us, in 1965 "after the forces of good had been wiped out".[124] And, if we need any further indication that this novel, and indeed the entire series, is to place politics very much in the foreground, we are immediately introduced to the major character who is attempting to escape to Iran. The escape party has been discovered, and one of them, an ex-police officer, has been shot in the back. The narrative present of the entire novel consists of conversations between the major character and the immobile police officer. It is worthy of mention at this point that the lack of names for many of the important characters in the first three novels serves at least two functions. In the first place, it allows the author to deprive the character of a specific identity as a person and to turn him into something akin to a type, almost a case-study within the many possible classes and attitudes of the society as a whole. Secondly, it forces the narrative to proceed on an impersonal and anonymous level which contributes in no small way to the generally sinister and oppressive atmosphere.

The police-officer's wound gradually putrefies, and he comes to realise that he is going to die. He asks the major character to bury him when he dies, and that permits the latter to remind the officer in forceful terms of his past crimes against humanity. This process not only reveals the tension between the two men hiding from the outside world in a tiny hut, but also allows Ismā'īl to vent his authorial spleen "after the forces of good had been wiped out".

However, these conversations have another, more important function within the framework of the novel as a whole: they serve to trigger off memories of the past in the mind of the major character which are our chief source of insight into his motivations. This trigger mechanism, the switching from present to past and *vice versa*, is a prominent feature of all four novels, and is handled with considerable skill. Through the use of different type-faces in the Arabic, Ismā'īl is able to operate on

[124] *Kānat al-samā' zarqā'*, 4.

a number of levels simultaneously: the narrative present, memories of the past (both narrative and dialogue), interior monologue and stream-of-consciousness. The transition between the different levels is also handled with great care, as in the following example:

"So you're going to abandon me here when I die?"
"You'll do that to yourself before I do".
"I'll go to hell," said the officer with a certain resignation, "isn't that how it is?"
"I don't think so."
"But I'm a murderer!"
"Murdered too."
"Do you believe in the Day of Judgment?"
"The way it's happened to you?"
A laugh from the corner of the hut.
"Is that all?"
"I want you to die a believer."
"Why?"
"Because you're human."
"What about you?"
The words "I'm not human," almost escaped from his lips. *The blue sledge-hammer started working inside his head. "You're not human," she had said. He could still hear that voice which was now sullied by a display of affection, "You're not human." ... "Those words of yours aren't a sufficient excuse for having emotions of stone when faced with a situation like this".*[125]

This passage not only serves to illustrate the way in which the author transfers the reader from one time to another (which we have duplicated in English type by the use of italics for the retrospect), but also introduces us to the primary focus of these memories, the relationship of the major character with two women. One of them is his wife, whom his father forced him to marry in order to put an end to an adolescent dalliance with another girl. The marriage is a failure, but his wife is pregnant; he has decided not to divorce her until the children are older. This is the "situation" referred to in the above quotation. The speaker is the second woman who, it emerges much later in the work, is distantly related to him and whose love for him stirs up a crisis in his consciousness and illustrates his vacillation. She is "the girl in the blue dress", continuing the colour image of blue found both in the title and the quotation above. The development of the affair between the two characters and the break-up

[125] *Ibid.*, 78-9.

of his marriage are narrated and analysed against the background of a Charlie Chaplin film which the major character is watching in a cinema with "the girl in the blue dress". The juxtaposition of the absurd antics of Chaplin and the irrational vacillations of the major character makes its point with great clarity, and to it is added the insistent questioning by the girl who becomes personified as "the blue dress" at the climax of his recollection of the break-up of his marriage, when his wife throws herself down in the middle of the street.[126]

In a desperate attempt to prevent him from going to Iran, the girl gives herself to him, after which, in another cutting comparison, he likens her walk to that of Charlie Chaplin. Switching back to the hut, even the dying officer finds his lack of humanity repulsive. Changing his mind yet again, the major character decides that he will go back to the girl:

> There was a smile on the officer's face. "Really?!" he asked joyfully. "When?"
> "Not before you die!"
> A feeble laugh emerged from the officer's mouth.[127]

We are to learn the sequel to these events in the fourth novel.

Ismāʿīl's commitment to illustrating some of the social tensions and conflicts of the 1960s is made apparent in a comment which prefaces the second of these novels, *al-Mustanqaʿāt al-ḍawʾiyya*. The work is dedicated to "the humanity of two people who lived through my death and participated in my birth, Jaʿfar Mūsā ʿAlī and Jamīl Jāsim al-Shabībī".[128] The "light-swamps" of the title are prison cells in which shafts of light will periodically penetrate the vile, foetid atmosphere. Using the same techniques as we have described with reference to the first novel, Ismāʿīl introduces the reader to a narrative present in which the major character (who has a name this time: Ḥumayda) is a prisoner serving a life sentence with hard labour. He has befriended the chief warder and other prison guards, and is thereby accorded a number of privileges. We are also made aware at the outset of the novel that his wife has married his closest friend, somewhat replicating the situation of Manṣūr Bāhī in Najīb Maḥfūẓ's novel *Mīrāmār*.[129] Once again, we learn

126 *Ibid.*, 94.
127 *Ibid.*, 142.
128 Beirut: Dar al-ʿAwda, 1971, 1973, 5.
129 *Mīrāmār*, 139 ff. Ismāʿīl appears to be an admirer of Maḥfūẓ in that he mentions his name twice in *Kānat al-samāʾ zarqā*, 132, 140.

the reason for his imprisonment in retrospect. Emerging from a cinema with his wife a few years earlier (the film had been by Alfred Hitchcock), he had witnessed the brutal murder by two men of their sister who had become a prostitute. This is a *crime d'honneur* which inevitably calls to mind the eloquent poem by the Iraqi poetess, Nāzik al-Malā'ika, *Ghaslan li-al-'ār* ("Washing away dishonour"):

> A last gasp through her teeth and tears.
> The vociferous moan of the night.
> Blood gushed.
> Her body staggered.
> The waves of her hair
> Swayed with crimson mud.[130]

While his wife watches in horror, Ḥumayda wades into the fray and kills both brothers in self-defence when they come at him with their knives. Public sympathy at his trial is with the brothers who were preserving the honour of their family, and, after the press vilifies him as a public menace, he is sent to prison for life.

The recollection of this incident is set against another like it in prison. Ḥumayda, the friend of the warder and prison guards, intercedes in a fight between two guards over cheating in a game. In contrast to the major character in *Kānat al-samā' zarqā'*, he is unable to prevent himself from making rapid decisions in a crisis, even at his own expense. The reader has now been introduced to two such cases: the result in one is life imprisonment, and in the other, solitary confinement.

This novel takes us full cycle; the final chapter begins with precisely the same description as the second: Ḥumayda cracking stones in the heat of the midday sun. There has, however, been a change. The old prison governor who admired his political writings (and encouraged him to continue them in prison under the pseudonym of Jāsim Ṣāliḥ) has been replaced by a much less sympathetic person, whose hatred of Ḥumayda as Jāsim Ṣāliḥ is so intense that he almost strikes him. But Ḥumayda's friend, the chief warder, intervenes.

The unnamed hero of the third novel, *al-Ḥabl*, is a leftist, although he has never joined the party. The narrative present in

[130] *Qarārat al-mawj*, Beirut, 1957, 158; trans. Kamal Boullata in *Women of the Fertile Crescent*, Washington: Three Continents Press, 1978, 20. Compare *al-Mustanqa'āt al-ḍaw'iyya*, 28-9.

the work takes place entirely within the space of a single night, as he proceeds to burgle the house of a police officer. Within this fabric, we learn through the consciousness of the protagonist what is the sequence of events which has brought him to his current position:

> A single poem, that's your entire life, just one poem. And with every succeeding burglary your poem loses another line. I wonder if the supply has run out. How many times have you challenged yourself to write another poem?! But now the only person you can find to lampoon is your own wife because she refuses to participate or even empathise with your stealing. Poetry ... revolution ... the left wing ... If only the revolution, the left ... In the old days thieves used to have their right hand cut off. Now it's the political left which has been severed.[131]

The significance of this "poem" is that it was against ʿAbd al-Karīm Qāsim who, until his bloody assassination, ruled Iraq with an iron hand in the 1960s. After spending six months in jail during which all attempts to link him with the party fail, he emerges allegedly a free (and innocent) man. He soon discovers, however, that he has lost his job and furthermore cannot leave the country, both because he is regarded as "a dangerous political extremist". In desperation, he makes his way to Kuwait on foot simply in order to earn a living for his wife and himself. After making some money and buying gifts for his wife, he is returned to Iraq by the Kuwaiti authorities because he has no passport. At the border post, everything he has earned and bought is taken from him, and at this point he decides to begin a career of burglary, stealing only from police officers' houses. All of this, spread over twelve chapters, explains the situation of the major character in the present which he narrates to the reader.

A number of other elements impinge upon the major character's thoughts as he makes his way painstakingly towards his target house for the night, avoiding policemen and guards of various kinds on the way. In the first place, there is his father, who beats him black and blue with a saucepan as a child and forces him to run away from home at the age of ten. Then there is his wife, who strives to make ends meet by doing sewing work but who emerges with regard to her husband as frustrated and not a little uninterested in his activities. Quite the opposite

[131] Beirut: Dār al-ʿAwda, 1972, 25.

is the maid in one of the houses which he proposes to rob who serves him in two ways: she provides him with useful information about the house and its owners (his original intention in getting to know her), and gratifies his sexual urges with a remarkable lack of restraint, thereby triggering a certain amount of guilt feeling towards his wife.[132]

The robbery itself proceeds according to plan in that he finds jewels and perfumes. However, in leaving he disturbs the child of the family and in lulling her back to sleep brings back yet another host of childhood memories of his own. Leaving everything that he has taken on the child's pillow, he makes his way home with a token twenty dinars, precisely the amount removed from him by the border guards when he returned from Kuwait.

Of all the three novels which we have discussed thus far, it is *al-Ḥabl* which shows the greatest mastery of the process of integrating the different layers of time and consciousness into a single artistic whole. Within the time frame, the novel takes us back to the major character's childhood, to his time in prison, to his married life in general, and to his investigation of the particular house where the maid lives, all these memories triggered by thoughts and occurrences during a single night of theft. While the local carpenter's horseshoe becomes a symbol of what is unattainable by a poor child during his youth (unless, that is, he resorts to stealing), the rope of the title is not only the means by which the burglar gains entry to the houses from which he wishes to steal but is also a symbol of the desire of his wife and himself for a normal life unaffected by "the single poem" which he wrote, a life in which they could afford to have a clothes-line of their own on the roof. Their quest is merely for "work and dignity".[133] At the conclusion of the novel, it is suggested that the wife may be getting her way in that he will give up burglary, but, as in the other two novels, the outcome is left hanging.

We quoted above Ismāʿīl's own words concerning the overall structure of this quartet of novels, in which he said that *al-Ḍifāf al-ukhrā*, the last in the series, is an attempt to follow up on *some* of the characters in the other three works (my emphasis). Bearing in mind our opinion stated above that the major

132 *Ibid.*, 73.
133 Ilyās Khūrī, *Tajribat al-baḥth ʿan ufq*, 95.

character in *al-Ḥabl* is the most fully-rounded and developed character in the first three works, it is perhaps significant that he alone of the three major characters finds his way into the fourth novel as a protagonist. Indeed he is now named as Kāẓim ʿAbīd. From the other two novels, Ismāʿīl takes the figures of Fāṭima, the girlfriend (and now wife) of the hero of *Kānat al-samāʾ zarqāʾ* who, after abandoning his decision to flee to Iran for a short period, has fled once again leaving her with his child by his first marriage; and of "the Visitor", none other than the chief warder in the prison where Ḥumayda was serving his life sentence in *al-Mustanqaʿāt al-ḍawʾiyya*. To this trio is added a "guest character" (to use the author's terminology), Karīm al-Baṣrī, whose role is derived "to some extent from the character Karīm al-Nāṣirī, the hero of *al-Washm*, a novel by the Iraqi writer, ʿAbd al-Raḥmān Majīd al-Rabīʿī".[134]

The setting in which the author's "single developing sequence of time" is to take place is described for us immediately in a series of staccato phrases:

Work, workers, the factory, the outskirts of the city, the fence, machines, noise, 1,200 workers, work hours, work conditions, pay.[135]

This terse accumulation of phrases serves as a sufficient prelude for the planning of a workers' strike which forms the background to this novel, while the reaction of the various characters to the situation tells us a great deal about their social and political attitudes. The circumstances are laid out for the reader first by Fāṭima, who is employed as the factory director's secretary, and she is followed by Kāẓim ʿAbīd who, having now given up a life of burglary, has found a job as a worker in the factory. The "newcomer", Karīm al-Baṣrī, is next; like Kāẓim he too has served time in prison, but has secured himself a somewhat more senior position as store superintendent. Lastly, we hear the version of "the Visitor", the chief warder who, after losing his job in the prison, is appointed *farrāsh* (a general factotum cleaner and messenger) to the director's office.

Each of these four characters reveals through his narrative the atmosphere of suspicion and fear which prevails. This is aided and abetted by the actions of the director. Not only does he arouse the suspicions of the workers and his staff by

134 *al-Ḍifāf al-ukhrā*, 7.
135 *Ibid.*, 9.

appointing the ex-prison warder as his *farrāsh*, but, once it is known that a strike is being planned, he dangles the possibility of a promotion in front of Karīm al-Baṣrī in order to get him to spy on the workers and find out their plans. Furthermore, the director triggers off the main events of the novel by dictating a letter to Fāṭima which is to go to the authorities; in it he reports that a strike is being planned and that three workers, Aḥmad ʿAbdallāh, Jaʿfar ʿAlī and Kāẓim ʿAbīd, should be arrested immediately. Fāṭima and Karīm react to this in different ways. Fāṭima is constrained by the fact that she must stay at her desk until it is time to go home, added to which is the problem that as a woman her social mobility is somewhat restricted. Kārim heads for "a cheap bar with lousy *ʿaraq*" to consider his dilemma: to cooperate with the director and gain a promotion, or to be true to his ideals and help his fellow-workers.[136] After getting well and truly drunk, he rushes off to Kāẓim's house and arrives just in time to notify him before the police arrive. Kāẓim escapes over the roof. The other two workers are not so fortunate and are arrested. Fāṭima meanwhile rushes away from work to inform the other workers, but arrives too late.

The place to which Kāẓim escapes is none other than Fāṭima's house. There he hides from the police and also witnesses (from a hiding place on the roof) Karīm's futile attempts to express his admiration for her. Fāṭima has in fact remained devoted to her husband, even though he has abandoned her for some unknown destination four years earlier.[137] While Karīm's advances disgust her, the presence of Kāẓim in the house arouses hidden feminine instincts inside her, but even in moments of desperation she compares him with her real husband.[138]

Kāẓim has proposed to the workers' strike council that he resume his career as a burglar in order to get some money for a strike fund; and what more appropriate place to start than the house of the director himself? The workers firmly reject the idea. In fact, they are deeply suspicious of the offers of support and help from Karīm and Kāẓim, both of whom are extremely annoyed by this implicit questioning of their commitment to the cause. Kāẓim discusses his idea with Fāṭima, and she too rejects

[136] *Ibid.*, 125. See also later, 224.
[137] E.g. *ibid.*, 16, 23, 39.
[138] *Ibid.*, 244.

it. In spite of all the opposition, he goes ahead with the plan and robs the director's house. He not only finds valuable jewels, but also manages to avoid arousing the "Visitor" (now also serving as the director's bodyguard), who continues to sleep soundly through the burglary.

At the end of the novel, Karīm al-Baṣrī has not only failed to gain the promotion for which he has acted with such fervent duplicity but has been fired by the director. He resorts yet again to his cheap bar and, after getting totally drunk, is arrested for accosting passers-by. Kāẓim resolves to go to Kuwait once again; he has had to endure the full force of Fāṭima's anger because his robbery has led to the arrest and torture of the "Visitor". In a parting gesture, he decides to take twenty dinars from the proceeds of the burglary for his "travel expenses".[139] Amongst all this dissipation and escapism, it is Fāṭima who seems to display the resolution. She begins to challenge her husband's hallowed statements as "great words, but just words; you were good at dealing with words, but that's all. These words need action. ..." And, in order to confirm her changing attitude, she asks herself the all-important question at the end of her section:

> I wonder what would happen if you came back now! I think I'd welcome you with the words: "How are you? Your son's grown up but he'll reject you too!"[140]

Before considering the qualities of the quartet of novels as a whole, some comments should be made about this fourth work as an attempt to pick up some threads from the first three and to follow a single narrative line with them. It is my opinion that the experiment is less than successful. In each of the first three novels the reader is aware that a strong political under-current pervades the work. The concentration on one major character and the author's rare ability to fuse elements of past, present and future into a single frame of consciousness both serve to produce a concentrated, if open-ended, experience; each novel merits a separate existence of its own. The fourth novel avoids repetition by concentrating (apart from Kāẓim) on ancillary characters from the earlier works, but unfortunately the author seems to allow his political agenda to insert itself too obtrusively into the narrative. After the subtle investigations of the

[139] *Ibid.*, 274.
[140] *Ibid.*, 282-3.

inner thoughts and aspirations of the characters in the first three works, the way in which opportunist and escapist are disposed of at the end of the last novel seems too neat and tidy. Indeed, their motivations which lead to the eventual conclusion are not a little predictable and obvious. And, by using in this last novel with so many "voices" the same narrative technique as in the other three, the author has not allowed himself to penetrate deeply into the mental processes of each character; even in a work which is twice as long as any of the others, there is simply not enough opportunity to do so. The overall result seems unfocused and contrived.

The above comments are concerned with the fourth novel both as a separate work and as a "capstone" for the entire quartet. I now turn to consider the merits of the earlier works and of those techniques which Ismāʿīl Fahd Ismāʿīl has used in this complex undertaking.

A significant place in any assessment of the impact of these works must be given to Ismāʿīl's use of language. Rare indeed are any excursions into a prolix narrative style in these novels; the emphasis is on short utterances, often in the form of exclamations or, on a more inward mental level, the terse cerebrations of the stream of consciousness. This technique is particularly obvious at the beginning of the novels where the reader is often left in a suspense of anonymity and mystery until the scattered segments of narrative begin gradually to provide a background against which to view the mental ramblings of the major character. From the stylistic point of view, it seems to be no accident that the comments on the back cover of the first novel come from three *poets*, ʿAbd al-Wahhāb al-Bayyātī, Ṣalāḥ ʿAbd al-Ṣabūr and—already quoted—ʿAbd al-Raḥmān al-Abnūdī. The language throughout remains a fully grammatical, standard written Arabic; in the rare occasions where he uses a colloquial word, it is placed within quotation marks and given a specific footnote.[141] The style which emerges, however, is no ordinary narrative prose; the extreme economy of diction which Ismāʿīl chooses as the best means of transmitting his multi-layered projection of the inner mind of his characters forces him to use his words with all the artistry of a prose poet or craftsman of the shortest of short stories.

It is this great talent of Ismāʿīl to use words to convey mood

141 *al-Ḥabl*, 13, 79.

as accurately and effectively as reality, and indeed to fuse the two together, which makes this series of novels such a notable contribution to the contemporary tradition of the Arabic novel. Nor should this literary estimate of their value leave unstated the fact that they provide from within a vivid portrait of Iraq during the 1960s. That is the stated goal of the author, and he achieves it with great distinction.

8. *Al-Nihāyāt*
ʿAbd al-Raḥmān Munīf

Recent structural analyses of a number of poems from the pre-Islamic period have shown with great clarity that the traditional notion that the *qaṣīda* possesses no unity of purpose can no longer be justified; these studies show clearly that the unifying thread which runs through these poems is based on a series of oppositions involving lack and the elimination of lack, of "plerosis" and "kenosis" (as used by Hamori in quoting Gaster).[142] To continue with Adnan Haydar, another student of this early Arabic poetry,

> The harshness of the desert, the constant movement of the tribe from place to place in search of herbage, the anxiety experienced as a result of this unstable life, the necessary severing of love and friendship ties, the belief in the relativity of all values, the strong indulgence in life, the bitter consciousness of the imminence of death, the heroic attempts to relive the happy moments of the past, and the necessary striving for the immortalization of those moments: all these are components of the pre-Islamic vision.[143]

These interpretations and others like them inevitably come to mind upon a first reading of the novel *al-Nihāyāt* ("Endings", 1978) by ʿAbd al-Raḥmān Munīf.[144] Consider the opening:

[142] See Andras Hamori, *On the art of medieval Arabic literature*, Princeton: Princeton University Press, 1964, 12.

[143] "The *Muʿallaqa* of Imru' al-Qays: its structure and meaning, I", *Edebiyat* II/2 (1977), 227-8.

[144] ʿAbd al-Raḥmān Munīf is a French-educated oil economist now resident in Baghdad, where he edits the journal *al-Nafṭ wa-al-tanmiya*. Novel writing is a spare-time activity for him. He has thus far published five novels: *al-Ashjār wa-ightiyāl Marzūq*, *Qiṣṣat ḥubb majūsiyya*, *Sharq al-Mutawassiṭ*, *Ḥīna taraknā al-jisr*, and *al-Nihāyāt*. He expresses a number of opinions about Arabic novels in general, and his own in particular, in *al-Maʿrifa* 204 (Feb. 1979), 188-99. See also Jabrā, *Yanābīʿ al-ruʾyā*, 36-40.

Drought! It was drought, again. During drought seasons, life and things change, even people. Their nature changes; sorrows come into being deep down inside the heart; initially they are vague, but when anger erupts—and that happens often—then they explode.[145]

The emphasis on the desert, intense heat, the dangers of travel, the search for food, all these features and others set this novel apart from others written in Arabic. Novels written by Arab authors have tended to a large degree to take as their subjects the city and its inhabitants and particularly the bourgeoisie, thus emulating at least the initial stages in the development of most of the Western novel traditions. There have, of course, also been novels which deal with life in the countryside, from the very early *Zaynab* of Haykal to ʿAbd al-Ḥakīm Qāsim's *Ayyām al-insān al-sabʿ* (see above pp. 120-31); there have also been novels, parts of which have been set in the desert, Ghassān Kanafānī's *Rijāl fī al-shams* (see above, pp. 68-9) for one. However, I am not aware of any other novel in Arabic which devotes its attention so unswervingly to a depiction of this particular segment of contemporary Arab society.

The setting of the novel is the village of al-Ṭība which is situated right on the edge of the desert. The hardships implicit in this rugged life serve to create strong bonds between the inhabitants of the village and also to bring back home in times of crisis those sons of the community who have decided to seek their fortunes elsewhere, and particularly in the "big city". It is in this metropolis that bureaucrats have been debating for some time whether or not to build a large earth dam near the site of the village in order to alleviate the more gruesome aspects of life during the hot season.

The major means by which the community survives is by hunting, although the more sensible members of the community realise that indiscriminate slaughter of birds and animals will work to their disadvantage. It is with this in mind that the villagers view with suspicion and resentment the groups of guests from the city who come out to the village in order to hunt for sport. As is the case with regard to the dam project, the city in this novel is something remote, often incomprehensible in its actions and inimical to the continued survival of the community.

This environment is depicted for the reader with tremendous

[145] Beirut: Dār al-Ādāb, 1978, 5.

care and skill, a point to which we shall return. But it may legitimately be asked at this point, who are the characters in the novel and what happens?

The principal character is the community as a whole. The actions of individuals are portrayed, but their import is seen within the framework of the larger picture, namely the village as a unit. Whatever characterisation they receive emerges from the description of their actions, and not from any attempt at internal analysis or still less from dialogue, of which there is comparatively little. In fact, the reader is supplied with only four names of characters in a work which covers one hundred and eighty-seven pages.

This then is very much a novel of environment, but that does not mean that there is no action at all. In fact, the manner in which a series of flashbacks recalling previous momentous occasions in the history of the village are recounted serves to lend the narrative certain elements of the folktale which are entirely appropriate to the situation of the novel. There is in fact a hero named ʿAssāf, a taciturn loner who is generally recognised to be the best hunter in the region and also the one person able to survive the worst caprices of the weather. He has often warned the villagers and their visitors about over-hunting the area, but his words have gone unheard. It is ironic therefore that, when four guests (*ḍuyūf*) arrive by car one day to hunt in the wake of a turbulent village meeting at which the ever-diminishing supply of game has been discussed, ʿAssāf agrees to take them far into the desert to a place which only he knows where these men stand a chance of finding some game to hunt. When they start hunting, the men shoot from a car while ʿAssāf walks in the morning sun with his ever-faithful hunting dog. His prowess as a hunter is proved when he manages to bag over twenty birds during the morning while the four men in the car can only catch five. As the sun rises higher in the sky, they all stop for lunch, In an insane gesture, the city sportsmen decide to resume hunting even though it is midday and, for some inexplicable reason, ʿAssāf agrees. Once again, he sets out on foot while the men ride in the car. A gigantic sandstorm comes up, and the entire group is marooned. Next day, a rescue party arrives to find the men in the car almost dead, but they soon recover when given food and drink. Not so ʿAssāf. After a prolonged search he is found almost buried by sand with his dog covering him to protect him from the vultures which are flying overhead; both are dead. When the sorrowful procession returns to the village, the whole community erupts into an expression of grief and anger. ʿAssāf's body is carried into the house of the Mukhtār, and a large number of the men of the village spent the entire night in a vigil over the body, telling a remarkable series of fourteen tales of varying lengths. Two of them are actually taken from the *Kitāb al-Ḥayawān* ("Book of animals") of al-Jāḥiẓ, but the context is completely appropriate since *all* the tales concern episodes involving animals, birds, dogs, goats, cats and gazelles. In the morning the village builder, Abū Zakū—who, as we are told sardonically, also builds graves—goes out to prepare for the burial ceremony. The final pages of the novel are devoted to a description of the funeral procession to the cemetery which involves not only the entire village and other villagers who have returned from the city for the occasion, but people from the entire surrounding area. As people split up to return to their homes following the burial, a group of men set off for the city to try once more to get the earth dam built, the measure which may help to ward off some of the more capricious attacks by nature on the village of al-Ṭība.

The individuals just described do indeed participate in this series of events in chronological order. However, we have suggested above that this is not a novel of individuals, but of a community in a constant struggle with the forces of nature. That this is the case becomes clearer when we consider the format of the work. Fully the first third of the book is taken up with a description of the village, its environs, its people and their perennial problems of sheer survival. Al-Ṭība, the major focus of the story, is mentioned in the first section (the chapters are unnumbered),[146] and its people are given a general characterisation in the second; in this latter regard, we learn a fact which is to be of some importance to the later stages of the work:

> The people of al-Ṭība know how to turn a tale in that remarkable way which makes things seem incredibly important; it's a trait which sons inherit from their fathers. In many people's opinion it makes them special kinds of people and even more gives them the ability to influence and even convince others.[147]

146 *Ibid.*, 11.
147 *Ibid.*, 13.

The third section brings us to the description of the physical environment:

Al-Ṭība is where the desert starts ... to the south, the ground gradually loses colour and limestone rocks can be seen. It changes by stages until you come close to the horizon, and then there are sand-dunes at first followed by the desert itself.

This emphasis on the impersonal aspects of the village and its surroundings continues for several chapters; we learn *en passant* that the events which are to follow must occur "after the War",[148] but for the purposes of this novel any further specificity of time (like that of characterisation) seems to be unnecessary. The unchanged and perhaps unchanging nature of the existence is thus given some almost unconscious emphasis. And then, following the description of a particularly crazed year of hunting, comes the first mention of any individual, namely ʿAssāf, at whose door the blame is laid for all this madness: "That big lunatic, ʿAssāf, he's responsible for all this misery!"[149] The following section describes ʿAssāf as the village sees him, along with his one-eyed dog.[150]

In the next section the time becomes more specific: "This year is unlike any other before it".[151] We are not told what year it is, but the situation has moved from an almost timeless description into the sequence of events which will bring the novel to its climax. The portents for a severe drought are all bad, and, to make things worse, the spring rains come very early and are of little use. As the situation gets worse, the villagers who have moved to the city send provisions of all kinds and eventually return themselves:

No sooner had their feet touched the soil of al-Ṭība and their eyes focused on its houses than they felt a profound sorrow; they chided themselves a great deal for staying away until now. Their consciences pricked them as they compared life in the city with life in al-Ṭība. But this sorrow and regret soon changed to a powerful desire to do something so that al-Ṭība might be saved this time and carry on till the dam was built.[152]

It is into this situation of transition from the general to the

148 *Ibid.*, 25.
149 *Ibid.*, 27.
150 *Ibid.*, 31.
151 *Ibid.*, 35.
152 *Ibid.*, 50.

specific in time and situation that the four guests come: "That very afternoon towards the end of summer, four guests arrived in two cars, along with friends of theirs from al-Ṭība." The stage is set for the series of events which take up the rest of the novel. When the hunting expedition returns to the village with the dead body of ʿAssāf and the men gather at the Mukhtār's house, the narrative mode changes again. Time is now frozen as the series of stories unfolds. However, these tales are not outside the general framework of the narrative in that they all concern animals and thus contribute to the general portrait of the villagers and their interests. In fact, several of them have a particular reference to the moral which is to be drawn from ʿAssāf's warnings when he was alive and from his unnecessary death. There is, for example, the story of a man who is frustrated one day when he fails to shoot a mountain goat. Next day he finds it again. He cannot understand why the animal is standing absolutely and uncharacteristically still. He shoots and immediately hears the animal scream. The sight that greets him however is unforgettable:

> With a final bound he reached the spot, but before he could even get a glimpse of the goat's horns, the little kid had poked its head and a tiny part of its body out of its mother. She was leaning over a little towards the right, but she kept trying with all the strength she had to push the new creature into the light of the world; she wanted to deliver it before she died. As she looked at it, her eyes were full of tears![153]

A similarly repugnant picture of wanton and needless destruction is provided by a story of the local Bey

> whose eyes were full of cruelty even when he laughed; and when he gave you a look of reproach or sarcasm, the feeling you got was one of fear mingled with a desire to run away.[154]

He brings to the village an open-backed truck with a swivel-chair mounted on it, and proceeds to use it to indulge in an orgy of killing.

> All the words in the world cannot describe the scene. The whine of bullets flying through the air created a terrifying, echoing orgy of sound in the broad expanse of the desert. The gazelles were running crazily in every direction, thus making a situation fraught with terror.

153 *Ibid.*, 117.
154 *Ibid.*, 160.

But the Bey was yelling with every salvo; he seemed almost drunk or insane.[155]

It is hardly surprising, after this succession of stories which display man's affection and admiration for animals, the traits which they show towards each other and even mankind, and his disgust at those who abuse and interfere with nature, that the death of ʿAssāf, who has all along warned them about such things and their consequences, now assumes proportions which turn his funeral into a collective purging of the community. Such is the emotion created by the all-night vigil, the return of so many of the village children from elsewhere and the arrival of people from the neighbouring regions that the village women, of whom absolutely nothing is heard throughout the work, appear at the grave site and begin a mournful chanting and dancing, all of which goes on "without any objection or interference from the men", as the narrator tells us.[156] As everyone returns to the village, a new resolve is in the air, and the departure of some of the men of the village for the city is a sign of it. In the Mukhtār's words:

If they agree to build the dam, I'll come back on a bulldozer to start the work myself. Then al-Ṭība will come to know the meaning of life instead of this death which it lives every single day.[157]

The men of the village have, of course, been to the city on this mission before. But as *al-Nihāyāt* ends, we are left with the strong impression that the effects of ʿAssāf's death are too powerful to allow the same thing to happen this time as has happened all the other times. Perhaps his death and its moral will at last bring some relief to the village and its struggling people.

155 *Ibid.*, 164.
156 *Ibid.*, 180.
157 *Ibid.*, 183.

CHAPTER V

CONCLUSION

In preparing the public lectures on which the present work has been based, the end of 1979 presented itself as the necessary *terminus ad quem*. At the very same time a conference on the Arabic novel was taking place in Fez, Morocco, the proceedings of which have since been published in *al-Ādāb*.[1] Several of the novelists whose works have been considered here participated in the conference: ʿAbd al-Raḥmān Munīf, Suhayl Idrīs, ʿAbd al-Karīm Ghallāb, Edward al-Kharrāṭ, ʿAbd al-Ḥakīm Qāsim and Ṣanʿallāh Ibrāhīm. A number of prominent critics were also in attendance. As might be expected, the scope of the papers at this conference ranged far and wide, and the discussions which followed were extremely lively. This was perhaps the more so because the situation of the conference in Morocco allowed certain writers who have often found themselves in political difficulties because of their beliefs and statements to attend and to address themselves in unequivocal terms to the issues of the novel and novelist within the context of contemporary Arab society. We have availed ourselves of these and other comments in preparing this expanded version of the original lectures.

In the preceding chapters, we have tried to trace the development of the novel genre in the Arab world and to show the ways in which it has carried out what Joseph Campbell terms "a courageous, open-eyed observation of the sickeningly broken configurations that abound before us, around us and within".[2] The current state of the novel genre within this broad geographical expanse suggests that, while the fortunes of certain national traditions may fluctuate in accordance with political and social circumstances, the genre as a whole continues to fulfill its function as a reflection of the variety and complexity of contemporary life in the region.

And what of the future? In surveying some of the most recent

[1] *al-Ādāb* (Feb.-March 1980), complete issue. The discussions are to be found in *al-Ādāb* (April-May 1980), 91-108.

[2] *The hero with a thousand faces*, Princeton: Princeton University Press, Bollingen Series XVII, 1949, 1968, 27.

ideological battles within Western literary criticism, Geoffrey Hartman notes that

Something has gone wrong—flamboyantly, interestingly wrong—with the idea of separate or hierarchical genres ... the issue is not the death of the novel but the freeing up of all kinds of prose.[3]

Joyce Carol Oates, the American novelist and critic, seems to reflect much the same feeling when she states that

I anticipate novels that are in fact prose poems; and novels that are written for the ear—to be "read aloud, silently".

I anticipate lyricism and airiness, luxuriant space, the freedom to attempt virtually anything within the elastic confines of the "novel"—and the privilege, perhaps unprecedented in literary history, of being as experimental as one wishes in the guise of being traditional or even readable.[4]

This introductory work has certainly shown that, while many Arabic novels continue to be conceived within relatively traditional frames, several writers have begun to move in significantly new directions. The elasticity of the genre's confines and the willingness, indeed the desire, of many Arab novelists to experiment with language are clearly evident in many of the works analysed in the previous chapter. The reference to "novels that are written for the ear" also brings to mind, within the context of Arabic literature, the ever-increasing interest among Arab littérateurs in the *Thousand and one nights* and other collections of popular narrative. As we saw in the first chapter, Jabrā Ibrāhīm Jabrā has been particularly forceful on this subject, and with that in mind, it is interesting to note that this famous collection of tales is discussed by several participants at the Fez conference within the context of modern fiction.[5] This trend is, of course, part of a larger process whereby Arab writers are searching back into the history of their narrative tradition for inspiration on both form and content: Jamāl al-Ghīṭānī uses Egyptian historical texts, ʿAbd al-Raḥmān Munīf cites extracts from al-Jāḥiẓ, and Jabrā couches his latest novel (*al-Baḥth ʿan Walīd Masʿūd*) within the frame of a tape-recording played back to a group of characters. This juxtaposition and even fusion of the very old and very new has been reflected in many of the finest novels to appear in the Arab world in recent

[3] *New York Times Book Review*, 5 April 1981, 11.
[4] *Ibid.*, 14 December 1980, 3.
[5] *al-Ādāb* (Feb.-March 1980), 106.

times. Such experimental combinations are symptomatic not only of the profound re-examination of both present and past in the light of the 1967 defeat and its aftermath, but also of the spirit of élan and even defiance with which Arab novelists deal with their present and look to their future.

Of all the creative writers who attended the conference in Fez, it was ironically Edward al-Kharrāṭ, that most cautious and self-critical of authors and more famous for his short stories at that, who gave the most detailed and personal description of the impulses which have made him a contributor to the tradition of the Arabic novel. The way in which his comments combine the particular situation of the Arab novelist with the general self-image of novelists on a world scale makes his comments an apt conclusion to our work:

Why do I write then? I write because I don't know why I write. Does the impulse come from some powerful force? I know that I use it as a weapon to bring about change, change both in the self and others ... for something better, more beautiful perhaps ... something warmer to ward off the bitter chill of barbarity and loneliness ... something soothing in the oppressive heat of violence and suffocation ... I write because I want there to be something in what I write—in everything I write—which will make even a single reader lift his head proudly and feel with me that in the end the world is not a desolate, meaningless landscape ... I write because the world's a riddle, woman is a riddle and so is my fellow man. All creation is a riddle ... that is what I want to write about, and that is why I write.[6]

[6] *Ibid.*, 110.

BIBLIOGRAPHY

1. THE NOVELISTS AND NOVELS

Note. This is a listing of novelists and works discussed in the text. It is not a complete listing of the novels of any author, nor does it include contributions to other genres (e.g. the novella or the short story). The date after each work is (as far as I have been able to determine) the date of original publication. For references to the text, consult the Index.

ʿAbbūd, Mārūn, *Fāris Aghā* (n.d.)
ʿAbdallāh, Yaḥyā al-Ṭāhir, *al-Ṭawq wa-al-aswira* (1975)
ʿAbd al-Quddūs, Iḥsān, *Anā ḥurra* (n.d. 1950s)
al-ʿAqqād, ʿAbbās Maḥmūd, *Sāra* (1938)
ʿAwwād, Tawfīq Yūsuf, *al-Raghīf* (1939)
Idem, *Ṭawāḥīn Bayrūt* (1972)
Ayyūb, Dhū al-Nūn, *al-Duktūr Ibrāhīm* (1939)
Idem, *al-Yad wa-al-arḍ wa-al-mā'* (1947)
Baʿalbakkī, Laylā, *Anā aḥyā* (1958)
Eadem, *al-Āliha al-mamsūkha* (1960)
Barakāt, Ḥalīm, *ʿAwdat al-ṭā'ir ilā al-baḥr* (1969)
Idem, *Sittat ayyām* (1961)
al-Dakhīl, Sulaymān, *Nāẓim Pāshā* (1911)
Farmān, Ghā'ib Ṭuʿma, *Khamsat aṣwāt* (1967)
Fayḍī, Sulaymān, *al-Riwāya al-īqāẓiyya* (1919)
Fayyāḍ, Tawfīq, *Majmūʿa 778* (1975)
Ghallāb, ʿAbd al-Karīm, *Dafannā al-māḍī* (1966)
Idem, *Sabʿat abwāb* (1965)
Ghānim, Fatḥī, *al-Jabal* (1957)
Idem, *al-Rajul alladhī faqada ẓillahu* (1960?)
al-Ghīṭānī, Jamāl, *al-Zīnī Barakāt* (1976)
Ḥabībī, Emile, *Sudāsiyyat al-ayyām al-sitta* (1969)
Idem, *al-Waqā'iʿ al-gharība fī ikhtifā' Saʿīd Abī al-Naḥs al-mutashā'il* (1974)
al-Ḥakīm, Tawfīq, *ʿAwdat al-rūḥ* (1933)
Idem, *ʿUṣfūr min al-sharq* (1938)
Idem, *Yawmiyyat nā'ib fī al-aryāf* (1937)
Haykal, Muḥammad Ḥusayn, *Zaynab* (1913)
Ḥusayn, Ṭāhā, *Adīb* (1935)
Idem, *al-Ayyām* (1926[1])

[1] Not strictly a novel, but discussed in the text for its qualities as a narrative.

Idem, *Shajarat al-bu's* (1944)
Ibrāhīm, Ṣan'allāh, *Tilka al-rā'iḥa* (1969)
Idem, *Najmat Aghustus* (n.d. 1970s)
Idrīs, Yūsuf, *al-Ḥarām* (1959)
Ismā'īl, Ismā'īl Fahd, *al-Ḍifāf al-ukhrā* (1973)
Idem, *al-Ḥabl* (n.d. 1972?)
Idem, *Kānat al-samā' zarqā'* (n.d. 1970?)
Idem, *al-Mustanqa'āt al-ḍaw'iyya* (1971)
Jabrā, Jabrā Ibrāhīm, *al-Baḥth 'an Walīd Mas'ūd* (1978)
Idem, *al-Safīna* (1969)
Jubrān, Jubrān Khalīl, *al-Ajniḥa al-mutakassira* (1908)
Idem, *al-Arwāḥ al-mutamarrida* (1908)
Kanafānī, Ghassān, *'Ā'id ila Ḥayfā* (1969)
Idem, *Mā tabaqqā lakum* (1966)
Idem, *Rijāl fī al-shams* (1963)
al-Khūrī, Colette, *Ayyām ma'ahu* (n.d. late 1950s?)
Lāshīn, Maḥmūd Ṭāhir, *Ḥawwā' bilā Ādam* (1934)
Maḥfūẓ, Najīb, *'Abath al-aqdār* (1939)
Idem, *Awlād ḥāratinā* (1959/1967)
Idem, *Bidāya wa-nihāya* (1951)
Idem, *al-Ḥubb wa-al-qinā'* (1979)
Idem, *al-Karnak* (1974)
Idem, *Khān al-Khalīlī* (1945)
Idem, *al-Liṣṣ wa-al-kilāb* (1961)
Idem, *al-Marāyā* (1972)
Idem, *Mīrāmār* (1967)
Idem, *al-Qāhira al-jadīda* (1946)
Idem, *al-Summān wa-al-kharīf* (1962)
Idem, *Tharthara fawq al-Nīl* (1966)
Idem, *al-Thulāthiyya* (1956-7) — *Bayn al-qaṣrayn* — *Qaṣr al-shawq* — *al-Sukkariyya*
Idem, *Zuqāq al-midaqq* (1947)
al-Māzinī, Ibrāhīm 'Abd al-Qādir, *Ibrāhīm al-Kātib* (1931)
Mīna, Ḥannā, *al-Maṣābīḥ al-zurq* (1954)
Idem, *al-Shirā' wa-al-'āṣifa* (1966)
Munīf, 'Abd al-Raḥmān, *al-Nihāyāt* (1978)
Na'īma, Mīkhā'īl, *Mudhakkirāt al-arqash* (1949)
Naṣrallāh, Emily, *Ṭuyūr Aylūl* (1962)
Qāsim, 'Abd al-Ḥakīm, *Ayyām al-insān al-sab'a* (1969)
Rabī', Mubārak, *Rifqat al-silāḥ wa-al-qamar* (1976)
al-Rabī'ī, 'Abd al-Raḥmān Majīd, *al-Washm* (n.d. 1960s?)
Ṣafadī, Muṭā', *Thā'ir muḥtarif* (1961)
Ṣāliḥ, al-Ṭayyib, *Mawsim al-hijra ilā al-shamāl* (1969)
al-Sayyid, Maḥmūd Aḥmad, *Fī sabīl al-zawāj* (1921)
al-Sharqāwī, 'Abd al-Raḥmān, *al-Arḍ* (1954)

Idem, *al-Fallāḥ* (1967)
Waṭṭār, al-Ṭāhir, *al-Zilzāl* (1974)
Zaydān, Jurjī, *Fatḥ al-Andalus* (1904)
Idem, *al-Ḥajjāj ibn Yūsuf* (1909)
Idem, *al-Inqilāb al-'Uthmānī* (1911)
Idem, *Istibdād al-Mamālīk* (1893)
Idem, *Ṣalāḥ al-Dīn* (1913)
al-Zayyāt, Laṭīfa, *al-Bāb al-maftūḥ* (1960)

2. TRANSLATIONS OF THE NOVELS

al-'Aqqad, 'Abbās Maḥmūd, *Sara*, tr. Mustafa Badawi, Cairo: GEBO, 1978.
'Awwād, Tawfīq Yūsuf, *Death in Beirut*, tr. Leslie McLoughlin, London: Heinemann, 1976.
Barakāt, Ḥalīm, *Days of dust ('Awdat al-Ṭā'ir...)* tr. Trevor Le Gassick, Wilmette, Illinois: Medina Press International, 1974.
Ghānim, Fatḥī, *The man who lost his shadow*, tr. Desmond Stewart, London: Heinemann, 1980.
Ḥabībī, Emile, *The luckless Palestinian*, tr. Salma al-Jayyusi and Trevor Le Gassick, New York: Vantage Press, 1982.
al-Ḥakīm, Tawfīq, *Bird from the East*, tr. R. Bayly Winder, Beirut: Khayat, 1966.
Idem, *The maze of justice*, tr. Aubrey S. Eban, London: The Harvill Press, 1947.
Ḥusayn, Ṭāhā, *An Egyptian childhood* tr. E.H. Paxton, London: Routledge and Sons, 1932; repr. Heinemann, London 1981.
Idem, *The call of the curlew (Du'ā' al-karawān)*, tr. A.B. as-Safi, Leiden: E.J. Brill, 1980.
Ibrāhīm, Ṣan'allāh, *The smell of it*, tr. Denys Johnson-Davies, London: Heinemann, 1971.
Jabrā, Jabrā Ibrāhīm, *The ship*, tr. Adnan Haydar and Roger Allen, Washington: Three Continents Press, 1982.
Jubrān, Jubrān Khalīl, *The broken wings*, tr. Anthony R. Ferris, New York: Citadel Press, 1957.
Idem, *Spirits rebellious*, tr. Anthony R. Ferris, New York: Philosophical Library, 1947.
Kanafānī, Ghassān, *Men in the sun*, tr. Hilary Kilpatrick, London: Heinemann, and Washington: Three Continents Press, 1978.
Maḥfūẓ, Najīb, *Children of Gebelawi (Awlād ḥāratinā)*, tr. Philip Stewart, London: Heinemann, and Washington: Three Continents Press, 1981.
Idem, *Midaq Alley*, tr. Trevor Le Gassick, London: Heinemann, and Washington: Three Continents Press, 1974.
Idem, *Mīrāmār*, tr. Fatma Moussa-Mahmoud, London: Heinemann, and Three Continents Press, 1978.

Idem, *Mirrors*, tr. Roger Allen, Chicago: Bibliotheca Islamica, 1977.
Al-Māzinī, Ibrāhīm, *Ibrahim the writer*, tr. Magdi Wahba, Cairo: GEBO, 1976.
Ṣāliḥ, al-Ṭayyib, *Season of migration to the North*, tr. Denys Johnson-Davies, Heinemann, 1970.
al-Sharqāwī, ʿAbd al-Raḥmān, *Egyptian earth*, tr. Desmond Stewart, Delhi: Hind Pocket Books, 1972.
The author is also aware of the existence of translations of the following novels as either being in process or completed. No dates of publication are available:
ʿAbd al-Quddūs, Iḥsān, *I am free*
Jabrā, Jabrā Ibrāhīm, *In search of Walīd Masʿūd*
Maḥfūẓ, Najīb, *Autumn quail*
Idem, *The search*
Idem, *The thief and the dogs*
Idem, *The trilogy*
(all part of a Maḥfūẓ novels translation project at the American University in Cairo Press)
Qāsim, ʿAbd al-Ḥakīm, *The seven days of man*

3. OTHER WORKS

i. *In Arabic*

Adūnīs (ʿAlī Aḥmad Saʿīd), *Zaman al-shiʿr*, Beirut: Dār al-ʿAwda, 1972.
ʿAfīfī, Muḥammad al-Ṣādiq, *al-Fann al-qaṣaṣī wa-al-masraḥī fī al-Maghrib al-ʿArabī 1900-1965*, n.p.: Dār al-Fikr, 1971.
Idem, *al-Qiṣṣa al-Maghribiyya al-ḥadītha*, Casablanca: Maktabat al-Waḥda al-ʿArabiyya, 1961.
al-ʿAlī Ṣāliḥ, *et. al.*, *al-Adab al-ʿArabī fī āthār al-dārisīna*, Beirut: Dār al-ʿIlm li-al-Malāyīn, 1971.
al-ʿAqqād, ʿAbbās Maḥmūd, *Ibn al-Rūmī: ḥayātuhu min shiʿrihi*, Cairo: Maṭbaʿat Ḥijāzī, 1938.
Idem, and Ibrāhīm al-Māzinī, *al-Dīwān*, Cairo: n.p. 1921.
al-Ashtar, ʿAbd al-Karīm, *Dirāsa fī adab al-nakba*, n.p. (Damascus?): Dār al-Fikr, 1975.
ʿAyyād, Shukrī, "al-Riwāya al-ʿArabiyya al-muʿāṣira wa-azmat al-ḍamīr al-ʿArabī", *Majallat ʿĀlam al-Fikr* III/3 (Nov.-Dec. 1972), 619-48.
Badr, ʿAbd al-Muḥsin Ṭāhā, *Najīb Maḥfūẓ: al-ruʾyā wa-al-adāt*, Cairo: Dār al-Thaqāfa li-al-ṭibāʿa wa-al-nashr, 1978.
Idem, *al-Riwāʾī wa-al-arḍ*, Cairo: al-Hayʾa al-Miṣriyya al-ʿĀmma li-al-Kitāb, 1971.

Idem, *Taṭawwur al-riwāya al-'Arabiyya al-ḥadītha fī Miṣr 1870-1938*, Cairo: Dār al-Ma'ārif, 1963.

Darrāj, Fayṣal, "al-Intāj al-riwā'ī wa-al-ṭalī'a al-adabiyya", *al-Karmal* I (Winter 1981), 118-43.

Duwwāra, Fu'ād, *Fī al-riwāya al-miṣriyya*, Cairo: Dār al-Kātib al-'Arabī, 1968.

Hādī, Fāḍil 'Abbās, "Qaḍiyyat Falasṭīn wa-al-riwāya al-'Arabiyya al-mu'āṣira", *Shu'ūn Falasṭīniyya* 11 (July 1972).

Ḥāfiẓ, Ṣabrī, "Azmat al-ḥurriyya fī al-riwāya al-mu'āṣira", *Ḥiwār* II/4 (May-June, 1964), 52-62.

Idem, "Bibliografiyā al-riwāya al-Miṣriyya 1876-1969", *Majallat al-Kitāb al-'Arabī* (July 1970).

Idem, "Ittijāhāt al-riwāya al-Miṣriyya ba'd al-thawra", *al-Majalla* 9 (July 1965), 102-11.

Ḥaqqī, Yaḥyā, *Fajr al-qiṣṣa al-Miṣriyya*, Cairo: al-Hay'a al-Miṣriyya al-'Āmma li-al-Kitāb, 1975.

Idem, *Qindīl Umm Hāshim*, Cairo: Dār al-Ma'ārif, 1944.

Ḥarb, Ṭalāl, "Fusḥat al-ikhtiyār: dirāsa bunyawiyya", *al-Ādāb* (July-Aug. 1980), 24-31.

Haykal, Aḥmad, *al-Adab al-qaṣaṣī wa-al-masraḥī min a'qāb thawra 1919 ilā qiyām al-ḥarb al-kubrā al-thāniya*, Cairo: Dār al-Ma'ārif, 1971.

Ḥusayn, Ṭāhā, *Mustaqbal al-thaqāfa fī Miṣr*, Cairo: n.p., 1938.

Ibn Dhurayl, 'Adnān, *al-Riwāya al-'Arabiyya al-Sūriyya*, Damascus: n.p., 1973.

'Izz al-Dīn, Yūsuf, *al-Riwāya fī al-'Irāq*, Cairo: Ma'had al-Dirāsāt al-'Arabiyya al-'Āliya, 1973.

Jabrā, Jabrā Ibrāhīm, *al-Ḥurriyya wa-al-ṭūfān*, Beirut: Dār Majallat Shi'r, 1960.

Idem, *al-Riḥla al-thāmina*, Sidon and Beirut: al-Maktaba al-'Aṣriyya, 1967.

Idem, *Yanābī' al-ru'yā*, Beirut: al-Mu'assasa al-'Arabiyya, 1979.

Kannūn, 'Abdallāh, *Aḥādīth 'an al-adab al-Maghribī al-ḥadīth*, Cairo: Ma'had al-Dirāsāt al-'Arabiyya al-'Āliya, 1964.

Khashaba, Sāmī, "al-Wāqi'iyya fī al-riwāya al-'Arabiyya al-mu'āṣira", *al-Ādāb* (May 1970), 11-12.

al-Khaṭīb, Ḥuṣām, *al-Riwāya al-Sūriyya fī marḥalat al-nuhūḍ*, Cairo: al-Munaẓẓama al-'Arabiyya li-al-Tarbiya wa-al-Thaqāfa wa-al-'Ulūm, 1975.

Khiḍr, 'Abbās, "al-Mūnūlūg al-dākhilī fī *Alf layla wa-layla*", *al-'Arabī* (Aug. 1980), 120-2.

Khiḍr, Su'ād, *al-Adab al-Jazā'irī al-mu'āṣir*, Beirut: al-Maktaba al-'Aṣriyya, 1967.

Khūrī, Ilyās, *Tajribat al-baḥth 'an ufq*, Beirut: P.L.O. Research Centre, 1974.

al-Ma'addāwī, Anwar, *Kalimāt fī al-adab*, Sidon and Beirut: al-Maktaba al-'Aṣriyya, 1966.

Māḍī, Shukrī ʿAzīz, *Inʿikās hazīmat Ḥazīrān ʿalā al-riwāya al-ʿArabiyya*, Beirut: al-Mu'assasa al-ʿArabiyya, 1978.

Muḥammadiyya, Ahmad Saʿīd *et al.*, *al-Ṭayyib Ṣāliḥ ʿabqarī al-riwāya al-ʿArabiyya*, Beirut: Dār al-ʿAwda, 1976.

al-Mūsawī, Muḥsin Jāsim, "Ḥawla mafhūmay al-shakhṣiyya wa-al-buṭūla fī al-riwāya al-ʿArabiyya al-muʿāṣira", *al-Mawqif al-Adabī* (Dec. 1979-Jan. 1980), 168-87.

Idem, *al-Mawqif al-thawrī fī al-riwāya al-ʿArabiyya al-muʿāṣira*, Baghdad: Wizārat al-Iʿlām, 1975.

al-Naḥḥās, Hāshim, *Najīb Maḥfūẓ ʿalā al-shāsha*, Cairo: al-Hay'a al-Miṣriyya al-ʿĀmma li-al-Kitāb, 1975.

al-Nāqūrī, Idrīs, "al-Shakl al-fannī fī al-riwāya al-maghribiyya", *al-Mawqif al-Adabī* (Dec. 1979-Jan. 1980), 40-63.

al-Rabīʿī, Maḥmūd, *Qirā'at al-riwāya*, Cairo: Dār al-Maʿārif, 1974.

al-Rāʿī, ʿAlī, *Dirāsāt fī al-riwāya al-Miṣriyya*, Cairo: al-Mu'assasa al-ʿĀmma li-al-Ta'līf wa-al-Tarjama wa-al-Ṭibāʿa wa-al-Nashr, n.d. 1964?

Saʿīd, Jamīl, *Naẓārāt fī al-ṭayyārāt al-adabiyya al-ḥadītha fī al-ʿIrāq*, Cairo: Maʿhad al-Dirāsāt al-ʿArabiyya al-ʿĀliya, 1954.

Saʿīd, Khālida, "al-Riwāya al-ʿArabiyya bayn 1920 wa-1972", *Mawāqif* 28 (Summer 1974), 75-88.

Sālim, Jūrj, *al-Mughāmara al-riwā'iyya*, Damascus: Manshūrāt Ittiḥād al-Kuttāb al-ʿArab, 1973.

al-Sharqāwī, Ḍiyā', "al-Miʿmār al-fannī fī riwāyat *al-Safīna*", *al-Maʿrifa* 193-4 (March-April 1978), 7-57.

Shawkat, Maḥmūd, *al-Fann al-qaṣaṣī fī al-adab al-ʿArabī al-ḥadīth*, Cairo: Dār al-Fikr, 1963.

al-Shītī, Sulaymān, *al-Ramz wa-al-ramziyya fī adab Najīb Maḥfūẓ*, Kuwait: al-Maṭbaʿa al-ʿAṣriyya, 1976.

Shukrī, Ghālī, *Azmat al-jins fī al-qiṣṣa al-ʿArabiyya*, Beirut: Dār al-Āfāq al-Jadīda, 1978.

Idem, *al-Muntamī: dirāsa fī adab Najīb Maḥfūẓ*, Cairo: Dār al-Maʿārif, 1969.

Idem, *al-Riwāya al-ʿArabiyya fī riḥlat al-ʿadhāb*, Cairo: ʿĀlam al-Kutub, 1971.

Ṭarābīshī, Jūrj, *Sharq wa-gharb rujūla wa-unūtha*, Beirut: Dār al-Ṭalīʿa, 1977.

al-Yāghī, ʿAbd al-Raḥmān, *al-Juhūd al-riwā'iyya*, Beirut: Dār al-ʿAwda, 1972.

Yāsīn, Bū ʿAlī, and Nabīl Sulaymān, *al-Adab wa-al-idīyūlūjiyā fī Sūriyyā 1967-1973*, Beirut: Dār Ibn Khaldūn, 1974.

ii. *In Western languages*

Abrams, M.J., *A glossary of literary terms*, New York: Holt, Rinehart and Winston, 1971.

Abu Deeb, Kamal, "The perplexity of the all-knowing", *Mundus Artium* X/1 (1977), 163-81.

Allen, Roger, "Egyptian drama and fiction in the 1970s", *Edebiyat* I/1 (1976), 219-33.

Idem, "*Hadith 'Isa ibn Hisham* by Muḥammad al-Muwailiḥī: A reconsideration", *JAL* I (1970), 88-108.

Idem, *Al-Muwayliḥī's Ḥadīth 'Īsā ibn Hishām. A study of Egypt during the British occupation*, Albany, New York: State University of New York Press, 1974.

Idem, "Some new Al-Muwailihi materials", *Humaniora Islamica* II (1974), 139-80.

Idem, "Some recent works of Najīb Maḥfūẓ", *JARCE* XIV (1977), 101-10.

Auerbach, Erich, *Mimesis: the representation of reality in Western literature*, Princeton: Princeton University Press, 1971.

Badawi, Mustafa, *A critical introduction to modern Arabic poetry*, Cambridge: Cambridge University Press, 1975.

Idem, "Commitment in contemporary Arabic literature", *Journal of World History* XIV/4 (1972), 858-79.

Idem, "Al-Māzinī the novelist", *JAL* IV (1973), 112-45.

Baker, Raymond William, *Egypt's uncertain revolution under Nasser and Sadat*, Cambridge, Mass.: Harvard University Press, 1978.

Barakat, Halim, "Arabic novels and social transformation", in *Studies in modern Arabic literature* ed. R.C. Ostle, Warminster: Aris and Phillips, 1975, 126-39.

Idem, *Visions of social reality in the contemporary Arab novel*, Washington: Center for Contemporary Arab Studies, Georgetown University, 1977.

Berque, Jacques, *Cultural expression in Arab society today*, Austin: University of Texas Press, 1978.

Booth, Wayne, *The rhetoric of fiction*, Chicago, University of Chicago Press, 1961.

Boullata, Issa J., "Encounter between East and West: a theme in contemporary Arabic novels", *MEJ* XXX/1 (Winter 1976), 44-62.

Connelly, Bridget, "The structure of four Bani Hilal tales", *JAL* IV (1973), 18-47.

Cox, R.G., ch. in *From Dickens to Hardy. The Pelican guide to English literature* VI, London: Pelican Books, 1958, 1960, 1963.

Critical perspectives on modern Arabic literature ed. Issa J. Boullata, Washington: Three Continents Press, 1980.

Culler, Jonathan, *Structuralist poetics*, Ithaca, New York: Cornell University Press, 1975.

Fernea, Elizabeth W. and B.Q. Bezirgan, *Middle Eastern Muslim women speak*, Austin: University of Texas Press, 1977.

Fernea, Robert, *Nubians in Egypt*, Austin: University of Texas Press, 1973.

Francis, Raymond, *Aspects de la littérature arabe contemporaine*, Beirut: Dar al-Maaref, Liban, 1963.

Forster, E.M., *Aspects of the novel*, London: Penguin, 1966.

Gibb, H.A.R., *Studies on the civilization of Islam*, London: Routledge and Kegan Paul, 1962 (originally in *Bulletin of the School of Oriental Studies* IV (1926-8), 745-60, V (1928-30), 311-22, 445-66. VII (1933-5), 1-22).

Gohlman, Susan, "Women as cultural symbols in Yaḥyā Ḥaqqī's *The Saint's Lamp*", *JAL* X (1979), 117-27.

Hafez, Sabri, "The Egyptian novel in the sixties", *JAL* VII (1976), 68-84.

Hamori, Andras, *On the art of medieval Arabic literature*, Princeton: Princeton University Press, 1974.

Haqqi, Yahya, *The Saint's lamp*, trans. Mustafa Badawi, Leiden: E.J. Brill, 1973.

Hāwī, Khalīl, *Kahlil Gibran, his background, character and works*, Beirut: American University in Beirut Oriental Series no. 41, 1963.

Hourani, Albert, *Arabic thought in the liberal age 1798-1939*, London: Oxford University Press, 1962.

Husayn, Tāhā, *The future of culture in Egypt* tr. Sidney Glazer, Washington: American Council of Learned Societies, 1954.

Iser, Wolfgang, *The implied reader: patterns of communication in prose fiction from Bunyan to Beckett*, Baltimore: Johns Hopkins University Press, 1974.

Jabrā, Jabrā Ibrāhīm, "Modern Arabic literature and the West", *JAL* II (1971), 76-91.

Jād, ʿAlī, "ʿAbd al-Raḥmān al-Sharqāwī's *al-Arḍ*", *JAL* VII (1976), 88-100.

al-Jayyusi, Salma, *Trends and movements in modern Arabic poetry*, Leiden: E.J. Brill, 1977.

Eadem, "Two types of hero in contemporary Arabic literature", *Mundus Artium* X/1 (1977) 35-49.

Jomier, J. "La vie d'une famille au Caire d'après trois romans de M. Naguib Mahfuz", *Mélanges de l'Institut Dominicain des Études Orientales* IV (1957).

Khulusi, Safa', "Modern Arabic fiction with special reference to Iraq", *Islamic Culture* XXX (1956), 199 ff.

Kilpatrick, Hilary, "The Arabic novel—a single tradition?" *JAL* V (1974), 93-107.

Eadem, "*Ḥawwā' bilā Ādam*: an Egyptian novel of the 1930s", *JAL* IV (1973), 48-56.

Eadem, *The modern Egyptian novel*, London: Ithaca Press, 1974.

Eadem, "Tradition and innovation in the fiction of Ghassān Kanafānī", *JAL* VII (1976), 53-64.

Knipp, C., "The *Arabian Nights* in England: Galland's translation and its successors", *JAL* V (1974), 44-54.

Kurd ʿAli, Muhammad, *Memoirs*, tr. Khalil Totah, Washington: American Council of Learned Societies, 1954.

Laroui, Abdallah, *The crisis of the Arab intellectual*, Berkeley: University of California Press, 1976.

Leavis, Q.D., *Fiction and the reading public*, London: Chatto and Windus, 1932.

Le Gassick, Trevor, "The literature of modern Egypt", *Books Abroad* XLVI/2 (Spring 1972), 232 ff.

Idem, "The luckless Palestinian", *MEJ* XXXIV/2 (Spring 1980), 215-23.

Idem, "A malaise in Cairo: three contemporary Egyptian authors", *MEJ* XXI/4 (Sept. 1967), 145-56.

Idem, "Some recent war-related fiction", *MEJ* XXV/4 (Sept. 1971), 491 ff.

Lukacs, Georg, *The theory of the novel*, Cambridge, Mass.: MIT Press, 1971.

Milson, Menahim, "Najib Mahfuz and the quest for meaning", *Arabica* XVII (June 1970), 155-86.

Idem, "Some aspects of the modern Egyptian novel", *Muslim World* XI/2 (July 1970), 237-46.

Miquel, André, "La technique du roman chez Neguib Mahfouz", *Arabica* X (1963), 74-89.

Modern Arab poets 1950-1975, tr. and ed. Issa J. Boullata, Washington: Three Continents Press, 1976.

Modern Arabic short stories, tr. Denys Johnson-Davies, London: Heinemann, and Washington: Three Continents Press, 1976.

Molan, Peter, "Sinbad the sailor, a commentary on the ethics of violence", *JAOS* XCVIII/3 (July-Sept., 1978), 237-47.

Moosa, Matti, "Naqqāsh and the rise of the native Arab theatre in Syria", *JAL* III (1972), 105-17.

Moosa-Mahmoud, Fatma, *The Arabic novel in Egypt*, Cairo: GEBO, 1973.

Naimy, Nadim, "The mind and thought of Khalil Gibran", *JAL* V (1974), 55-71.

Nasr, Ahmad A., "Popular Islam in al-Ṭayyib Ṣāliḥ", *JAL* XI (1980), 88-104.

Nijland, C. *Mikhail Nuʿaymah, promotor of the Arabic literary revival*, Istanbul: Netherlands Historisch-Archaeologisch Instituut te Istanbul, 1975.

Pantucek, Svetozar, *La littérature algérienne moderne*, Prague: Oriental Institute in Academia, 1969.

Philipp, Thomas, *Ǧurǧī Zaidān, his life and thought*, Beirut and Wiesbaden; Orient-Institut der DMG and Franz Steiner, 1979.

Rizzitano, Umberto, "Il 'racconto' (*qiṣṣah*) nella narrativa araba contemporanea del Marocco", *Atti del terzo congresso di studi arabi e islamici, Ravello*, Naples: Istituto Universitario Orientale di Napoli, 1967.

Sakkut, Hamdi, *The Egyptian novel and its main trends 1913-1952*, Cairo: American University in Cairo Press, 1971.

Scholes, Robert and Robert Kellogg, *The nature of narrative*, London: Oxford University Press, 1966.

Semah, David, *Four Egyptian literary critics*, Leiden: E.J. Brill, 1974.

Sharabi, Hisham, *Nationalism and revolution in the Arab world*, Princeton: Van Nostrand Co, 1966.

Siddiq, Muhammed, "The process of individuation in al-Tayyeb Salih's novel *Season of migration to the North*", *JAL* IX (1978), 67-104.

Smith, Charles, "Love, passion and class in the fiction of Muḥammad Ḥusayn Haykal", *JAOS* XCIX/2 (1979), 249-61.

Somekh, Sasson, *The changing rhythm*, Leiden: E.J. Brill, 1973.

Studies in modern Arabic literature, ed. R.C. Ostle, Warminster: Aris and Phillips, 1975.

The Study of the Middle East: research in the humanities and social sciences, ed. Leonard Binder, New York: John Wiley, 1976.

Trilling, Lionel, *The liberal imagination*, New York: Scribner, 1940 and 1950.

Vial, Charles, art. "Ḳiṣṣa", in *EI*², Leiden: E.J. Brill, 1954-, in progress.

Watt, Ian, *The rise of the novel*, London: Penguin, 1963.

Women of the Fertile Crescent: modern poetry by Arab women, ed. Kamal Boullata, Washington: Three Continents Press, 1978.

INDEX